W9-AEP-974

HUNTINGTON LIBRARY PUBLICATIONS

ROWLANDSON'S DRAWINGS FOR A TOUR IN A POST CHAISE

ROWLANDSON'S DRAWINGS FOR A TOUR IN A POST CHAISE

WITH AN INTRODUCTION AND NOTES BY ROBERT R. WARK

THE HUNTINGTON LIBRARY, SAN MARINO, CALIFORNIA

1964

LIBRARY OF CONGRESS CATALOGUE CARD NUMBER 62-18104
PRINTED BY ANDERSON, RITCHIE & SIMON
DESIGN BY WARD RITCHIE
Second Printing 1964

PREFACE

THE EXISTENCE and importance of the drawings for Rowlandson's "Tour in a Post Chaise" have been known to students since the first partial publication of the series by Joseph Grego in *The Graphic Summer Number* for 1891. During the interval, however, Paul Oppé (in the early 1920's) appears to have been the only scholar who had access to the originals. Other writers on Rowlandson have relied on Grego's account and the thirty-seven facsimiles of the drawings that were included with his article. The fact that the originals have been in the Huntington collection for about forty years appears to have been generally unknown. This book is the first complete publication of the drawings and the first serious attempt to deal with the numerous problems they present.

It is a pleasure to recall and acknowledge the generous assistance I have received in the course of research on Rowlandson's "Tour in a Post Chaise." I am particularly grateful to many local historians and other scholars for assistance with the numerous, rather specialized antiquarian questions raised by several of the drawings. Mr. A. T. Lloyd, of New Milton, has been most helpful in dealing with drawings of the Lymington area, as has Mr. H. de S. Shortt for those connected with Salisbury. Mr. M. S. Robinson, of the National Maritime Museum, has supplied valuable information about nautical questions, and Mr. C. H. Gibbs-Smith, of the Victoria and Albert Museum, has given me the benefit of his expert knowledge of the history of aeronautics. Professor E. K. Waterhouse read the complete manuscript and made many helpful suggestions. I also wish to thank Betty Leigh Merrell and members of the Huntington Library publications staff for assistance in preparing the manuscript for the press.

I owe a particular debt of gratitude to Mr. John Hayes, of the London Museum, in whose company I retraced the tour in September 1961. Mr. Hayes has generously shared his extensive knowledge of Rowlandson both in oral discussion and in his specific comments on the introduction to this book, which he read in typescript.

The publication of the book was made possible through the generosity of the trustees of the Henry E. Huntington Library and Art Gallery and the Friends of the Huntington Library.

ROBERT R. WARK

San Marino, California
January 1962

CONTENTS

SOME DATES IN THE LIFE OF THOMAS ROWLANDSON

1757 (or 1756) Thomas Rowlandson born on July 14 in the Old Jewry, London, son of a textile merchant, William Rowlandson.

1759 William Rowlandson declared bankrupt. Thomas placed in the care of his uncle and aunt, James and Jane Rowlandson.

1764 Death of James Rowlandson. Thomas left henceforth in the care of his aunt.

1772 Entered the Royal Academy Schools on November 6.

Mid-1770's Visited Paris for an undetermined length of time.

1775 First exhibited at the Royal Academy.

1784 Exhibited "Vauxhall" and "The Serpentine River"; September-October, probable time of the "Tour in a Post Chaise."

1786 Exhibited "An English Review" and "A French Review."

1787 Last exhibited at the Royal Academy.

1789 Death of Rowlandson's aunt, by whose will Rowlandson received approximately £2,000.

1789 Traveled with Henry Wigstead to Brighthelmstone (Brighton). Published a series of prints commemorating the trip, with text by Wigstead, in 1790.

1797 Traveled with Wigstead in north and south Wales. A book commemorating the journey was published in 1800.

Late 1790's Began association with the publisher Rudolph Ackermann, for whom Rowlandson executed a great quantity of graphic work throughout the remainder of his career. Also met one of his most consistent patrons, the banker Matthew Michell.

1800 Death of Wigstead.

1808-1811 *The Microcosm of London*, 3 vols., with colored plates by Rowlandson and Augustus Charles Pugin, published by Ackermann.

1812-1821 The three *Dr. Syntax* tours, with illustrations by Rowlandson and text by W. Combe, published by Ackermann.

1815-1816 *The English Dance of Death*, 2 vols., with illustrations by Rowlandson and text by W. Combe, published by Ackermann.

1827 Died on April 21. Buried in St. Paul's, Covent Garden.

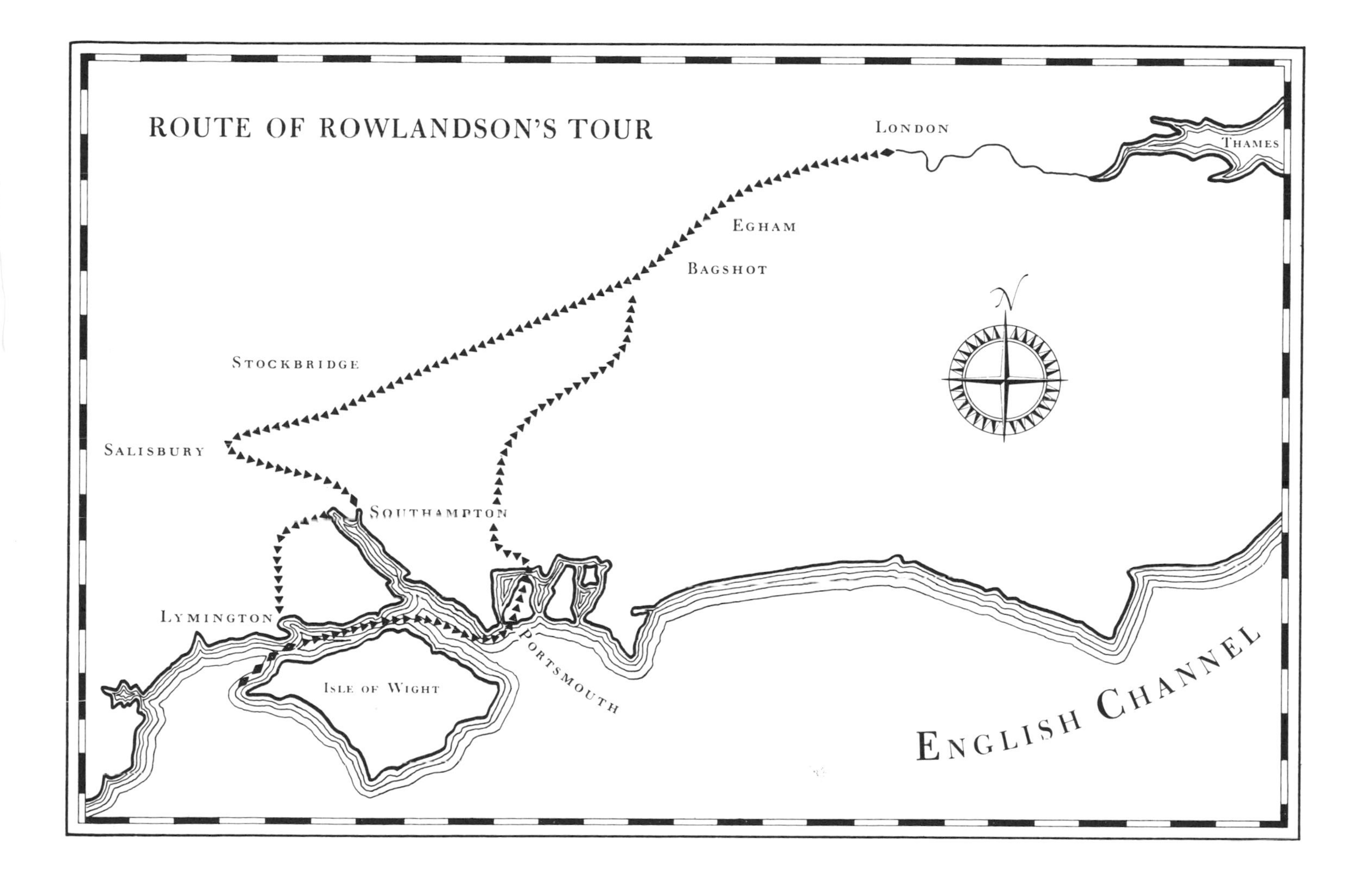
ROUTE OF ROWLANDSON'S TOUR
London
Thames
Egham
Bagshot
N
Stockbridge
Salisbury
Southampton
Lymington
Portsmouth
Isle of Wight
English Channel

WHEN Thomas Rowlandson made the tour recorded in the drawings here reproduced, he was in his mid-twenties, a gay young bachelor well started on a promising career. The tour itself was a rather madcap excursion undertaken in high good spirits, and the drawings made along the route are brimming with vitality. They are also the work of a surprisingly mature artist. Rowlandson's abilities as a draftsman are seldom more powerfully or happily displayed than in this youthful production.

It would be of great interest to learn more about Rowlandson's early years and the steps by which he arrived at the point where he could produce drawings such as these. Unfortunately, documents and information concerning his upbringing are scarce and not always completely reliable. There is uncertainty even about the year of his birth. The early biographical accounts (including the obituary notice in the *Gentleman's Magazine*) give the date as July 1756.[1] Rowlandson himself, however, when he entered the Royal Academy Schools on November 6, 1772, said that he was fifteen the previous July 14, thus placing his birthday in 1757.[2] Although one must allow a margin for error in either record, it would seem that Rowlandson's own statement should have priority.

The artist's father was a textile merchant who had the misfortune to go bankrupt in 1759.[3] Thomas was placed in the care of more prosperous relatives, and it was eventually a French Huguenot aunt, Jane Rowlandson (nee Chevalier), who brought up the boy and provided for his education.[4] She must have been a generous and warmhearted woman with a real affection for her nephew. Furthermore, she was reasonably well-off. Her husband, James Rowlandson, had also been in the textile business but was more fortunate financially than the artist's father. At James's death in 1764 he left his wife a modest fortune, about two thousand pounds of which eventually (in 1789) came to young Thomas. In the meantime, Jane sent her nephew to school to the establishment of Dr. Barvis in Soho Square and later (in 1772) to the Royal Academy Schools. During the 1770's Rowlandson also spent some time in Paris. It is not known precisely when or for how long he was there, but he was probably back in London by 1775, when he first

[1]*Gentleman's Magazine*, XCVII, Pt. 1 (1827), 564.

[2]From the "Students' Register of the Royal Academy Schools." Gilbert Davis has pointed out that the section of the register for the years 1769 to 1773 has been entered *en bloc* at some later date, and consequently there is more likelihood of error (see *Watercolors & Drawings by Thomas Rowlandson* [London: The Arts Council, 1950], p. 2).

[3]*Gentleman's Magazine*, XXIX (1759), 47.

[4]The most recent biographical study of Rowlandson and his family origins is embodied in Bernard Falk, *Thomas Rowlandson: His Life and Art* (London, [1949]).

exhibited at the Royal Academy. Rowlandson's name appears with considerable regularity in the catalogues of the academy exhibitions until 1787. He also displayed four drawings at the Society of Artists in 1783. None of his exhibits prior to 1784 is known to exist, although we have the names of a few of them. His earlier contributions were mostly small-scale full-length portraits, probably in water color. In 1784, however, he exhibited two of his acknowledged masterpieces, "Vauxhall" and "The Serpentine River," both of which fortunately survive.[5] With these productions he was already at full artistic maturity, working with the type of subject that was to remain his stock-in-trade for the rest of his career.

It was at about this time, when the world must have seemed a rather sunny place to young Rowlandson, that he set off on the tour recorded in the series of drawings now in the Huntington Library. He traveled with a friend and fellow artist, Henry Wigstead.

The details of Wigstead's biography are even fewer than those of Rowlandson's. We learn from his obituary notice in the *Gentleman's Magazine* that at the time of his death (September 29, 1800) Wigstead was a magistrate and clearly a man of some substance and property.[6] Part of his fortune came through his marriage. It is evident from the drawings in the Huntington series that he was older than Rowlandson. Possibly for this reason he seems to have been the treasurer on the journey. His appearance, simply as it emerges from the drawings, suggests a pleasant and relaxed person. The somewhat potbellied silhouette; the solicitous pose he assumes with his hands clasped behind his back under his coattails; the inclination to make friends: all this is comfortable and reassuring. Rowlandson appears boyish in comparison, with an exceedingly trim figure and a very clear propensity for pretty women.

It is probable that Wigstead was a family friend as well as a personal one. He lived for much of his life in Gerrard Street, Soho, near Rowlandson's home.[7] The fact that in 1785 Rowlandson's well-to-do aunt appointed Wigstead one of her executors indicates that she knew him well and had confidence in him.[8] For the last two years of his life he was a justice of the peace for Kensington, and this would further confirm that he was

[5]"Vauxhall" is in the collection of A. E. Pearson. The original of "The Serpentine River" is probably the drawing in the collection of Mrs. Brian Clutton; an early repetition is in the London Museum (see John Hayes, *A Catalogue of the Watercolour Drawings by Thomas Rowlandson in the London Museum* [London, 1960], No. 1).

[6]*Gentleman's Magazine*, LXX, Pt. 2 (1800), 1007-1008.

[7]Wigstead gave his address as 47 Gerrard Street, Soho, when exhibiting at the Academy.

[8]The codicil to Jane Rowlandson's will naming Henry Wigstead as a joint executor with her nephews Thomas Rowlandson and Samuel Chatellier is dated October 5, 1785.

a sober citizen of some stature.[9] But at the time of the early trip with Rowlandson he was certainly no kill-joy and entered into the fun with spirit and relish.

The pair made other trips (to Brighthelmstone [Brighton] in 1789 and to Wales in 1797), but the journey we are concerned with is the first of which there is any record. On the later occasions Wigstead wrote a commentary to accompany Rowlandson's drawings, and the two were published together. But if Wigstead left a journal of this first trip, it has now disappeared.

There was nothing unusual about the tour on which Rowlandson and Wigstead embarked. By the late eighteenth century, travel was almost as popular a pastime as it is now. Books describing various excursions of much the type undertaken by Rowlandson and Wigstead streamed from the printing presses, increasing in volume as the century progressed, to reach a veritable flood about 1800. There were many factors leading to this growing interest in travel, including such purely practical considerations as better roads. But also important was an increasing delight in natural scenery—and in a greater variety of natural scenery than had generally been enjoyed earlier. As the attitudes characteristic of the romantic temperament developed and prospered, travelers became more sensitive to the moods suggested by different types of landscape, ranging from the calm and idyllic to the turbulent and awesome. Nor was it only the mood of the scene that was explored. Artists in particular gave attention to such simple visual properties of landscape as light and color, textures and surfaces. Out of these varied concerns emerged, at the end of the eighteenth century and through the early nineteenth, the great English school of landscape painting.

It is doubtful if the exploration of landscape was the principal motive for Rowlandson's tour. To be sure, he did devote several drawings to the scenery around the western tip of the Isle of Wight. These are accurate topographically, with little of the sense of drama one might expect an artist to see in such rugged terrain. Clearly Rowlandson was primarily attracted simply by the picturesque irregularities of the contours and the play of light and shadow over the rocks. But his dominant interest in the series, as throughout his career, was with people and situations rather than scenery. Rowlandson did, in fact, remain generally oblivious to the great developments that took place in the study, description, and painting of English landscape during his lifetime. The spirit in which he and Wigstead undertook their tour reminds one forcibly of that of Hogarth and his friends on their famous "Five Days' Peregrination" in 1732.[10]

[9] Wigstead's appointment as justice of the peace for Kensington is dated May 22, 1798. The document is in the Middlesex County Record Office in "Oaths Taken by Justices of the Peace October 1789 to February 1804," p. 127.

[10] See Charles Mitchell, *Hogarth's Peregrination* (Oxford, 1952).

The primary motive on both occasions was nothing more nor less than fun—and fun of a rather raucous kind. Rowlandson and Wigstead traveled in much greater state than Hogarth and his friends, and the whole journey was a more elaborately planned affair, but the mood of the two is very similar. And the relation may not be accidental. Rowlandson knew the original manuscript record of Hogarth's "Peregrination" and made a copy of it (probably in 1781), which is now in the British Museum.[11] It appears possible that he may also have had a hand in preparing the plates for the first printing of the "Peregrination" in 1782.

We do not know the precise circumstances surrounding Rowlandson's tour. We cannot be certain when the trip took place, what route was followed, or if some special situation prompted the journey. In all these respects (and several others) the drawings have the fascination of a detective story, with Rowlandson liberally sprinkling clues throughout the series. Unfortunately, however, there is no final recapitulation by Rowlandson in which we can correct or test our powers of deduction and be told how foolish we have been. Of course Rowlandson himself was certainly not responsible for the puzzle element; this has become prominent primarily because of what has happened to the drawings during the century and three quarters since they were created.

The drawings appear to have been lost to sight for about a hundred years. They first emerge in the third day of the Thomas Capron sale (Christie's, January 20, 1888, Lots 385-408 [67 drawings in 24 lots]). The catalogue entry under the Rowlandson section reads: "The following Drawings form a Tour made with his friend Wigstead in 1783 or 1784 and have never been published." In the sale the drawings were capriciously grouped from the point of view of order. It is clear that they were not then bound in any sort of book, nor is there indication of any manuscript commentary with them.

When we next hear of the drawings, they are in the possession of that indefatigable student of Rowlandson, Joseph Grego. As Grego makes no mention of them in his great two-volume compendium *Rowlandson the Caricaturist*, published in 1880, it is fairly safe to assume that he did not know the drawings at that time, nor were they then in the Capron collection.[12] But Grego exhibited some of them as from his own collection in the large Naval Exhibition of 1891 (Nos. 1698-1702). Also in 1891 there appeared in *The Graphic Summer Number* an article describing the drawings, with thirty-seven of them reproduced in color facsimile. The drawings are spoken of as "lately discovered." The article, signed "J. G.," is certainly by Grego, and has remained

[11]See A. Paul Oppé, *The Drawings of William Hogarth* (London, 1948), No. 29.

[12]Grego, *Rowlandson the Caricaturist* (London, 1880), II, 425-426.

until the present the most important source of information about the sketches.

It is immediately clear from reading this article in the *Graphic* that Grego had available some data concerning the drawings that has subsequently disappeared. He frequently provides, from no apparent source, titles that are both too specific and (on investigation) too accurate to be chance suggestions on his part. He discusses the drawings in an order different from that in which they were sold at the Capron sale and also different from that in which they were bound when they entered the Huntington collection; and Grego's order makes much the best sense from the point of view of the itinerary probably followed. For all these reasons the 1891 article is an important source of information about the drawings, and accordingly the full text of Grego's commentary has been printed as an appendix to the present book. Unfortunately there are also some patent errors in Grego's account, so while it is a source of great value, it cannot be relied on implicitly.

By 1921 the drawings had come into the possession of William Henry Bruton, and they were sold in that year with his collection at Sotheby's on June 10 (Lot 328). At that time they were purchased by the Philadelphia bookdealer Charles Sessler, from whom Mr. Huntington acquired them early in 1925. The description of the drawings in the Bruton sale catalogue makes it clear that they were already mounted in the handsome green morocco Rivière covers in which they entered the Huntington collection.

The job of mounting and binding was carefully done and has doubtless served as an invaluable protection for the drawings, but it has vastly complicated the problem of dealing with them. In the first place, they have all been very firmly pasted down on cardboard mounts. But unfortunately no record was made of what is on the backs of the drawings. Unquestionably there is writing on the backs of some, and there are drawings on the backs of others. Both drawings and writing appear to be in Rowlandson's hand, and all are related to episodes shortly prior to or on the tour. It has been possible with various types of photography to read and interpret some of this material, but the results are agonizingly incomplete. Nevertheless, such information as can be derived from the backs provides strong confirmation for the normal assumption that the drawings originally formed a sketchbook. Although the drawings have been trimmed, presumably at the time they were mounted, the narrow range of variation in size suggests that not much has been lost; none of the 1891 facsimiles show more of a drawing than we now have. But it is also clear, from remnants of writing, that in some instances inscriptions on the fronts of the drawings have been cut off.

When the drawings were mounted, titles were supplied on the mounts. The captions follow very closely those given by Grego to the sketches he reproduced. But as the thirty he did not include are also given titles that are equally explicit, it is clear that Grego's article was not the source from which they were derived. Some are actually written on the drawings in Rowlandson's hand, and others have probably been trimmed off; the rest may have been constructed from the comments on the backs. Here again, however, although most of the titles that have been supplied prove to be accurate, they are not invariably so and must be handled with some caution. Moreover, at the time the drawings were mounted, the order was changed somewhat from that given by Grego, and the changes are almost certainly errors as far as the route probably followed by the travelers is concerned.

The situation for anyone dealing with the drawings is thus highly tantalizing. There is a considerable amount of information associated with them, but it obviously does not provide us with the whole story, nor is it always completely accurate and reliable in the details it does supply.

Of the various puzzles that confront the student studying the drawings, probably the one that can be solved most simply involves the route taken by the travelers. The places represented in several of the early drawings are clearly identified in Rowlandson's own hand. Thus with the aid of contemporary road maps and guidebooks it is not difficult to determine the route being followed, and thereafter the whole journey falls readily into place. The travelers started out on the main road from London to Exeter and Land's End, which they followed to Salisbury. They set off, like most travelers in the eighteenth century, at an early hour. Rowlandson's housekeeper roused him out of bed at four in the morning. By seven the post chaise had reached Hounslow, but the travelers went on about eight miles further to Egham before having breakfast. They continued through Bagshot to Hook, a little under forty-three miles from London and just over halfway to Salisbury. From Hook the road went to Basingstoke, where there was a choice of routes to Salisbury: a northerly one through Whitchurch and Andover and a southerly one through Popham Lane and Stockbridge. They chose the second, which (according to John Cary's *New Itinerary* of 1798) was slightly shorter. In spite of an accident in the early afternoon at Popham Lane, the travelers would easily make Salisbury by nightfall of their first day out.

They must have remained at Salisbury at least a couple of days, visiting the sights of the vicinity (particularly the cathedral, Wilton House, and Stonehenge) before they moved on to Southampton. As there are no drawings for the portion of the trip between Salisbury and Southampton, we cannot be sure which of the many possible routes they took, although the reference to Romsey on the back of one drawing suggests they went through that town. After at least one night at Southampton, they traveled on through Lyndhurst and the New Forest to Lymington. This last town appears to have been the principal stop on the tour. Judging from the number of drawings Rowlandson has left us of the vicinity, he and Wigstead must have spent several days there, making friends, seeing the sights, and generally enjoying themselves. Just why they chose to stay at Lymington is not clear. From all accounts it was a pleasant but not particularly unusual small town. The sea baths (of which Rowlandson has left us a drawing) were attracting some attention from visitors, but the place could hardly be considered a resort. Probably the most distinguished local inhabitant at the time was that high priest of the picturesque, William Gilpin, the vicar of Boldre, whose parish included Lymington. It is just possible that the clerical gentleman who figures as a friend of Wigstead in two of the drawings (Nos. 34 and 43) may be Gilpin. Certainly Wigstead's own later essays on picturesque travel suggest that the two men would have much in common.

From Lymington Rowlandson and Wigstead traveled by boat across the Solent to the Isle of Wight. Rowlandson was clearly fascinated by the scenery on the western tip of the island around The Needles and made a whole series of sketches of the area. The only town they appear to have visited on the island was Cowes, where they probably spent a night. From there they again took a boat across Spithead to Portsmouth. After a day or two at Portsmouth, during which they visited a man-of-war in the harbor and saw the wreck of the *Royal George*, they started on their homeward journey. Either Rowlandson was becoming a little bored or we have lost some of his drawings, but in any event the last leg of the trip is much the least well documented. Apparently the travelers did not visit Winchester but took a more direct, well-established road to London through Alton, Farnham, and probably Farnborough, rejoining the road they had taken out near Bagshot.

The duration of the trip must have been about twelve days. Wigstead's parting comment to his wife was, "You may expect to see me again Sunday Sennight" (drawing No. 6). If one is correct in interpreting "Sunday Sennight" to mean a week from Sunday, then the trip was expected to last something between one and two weeks. The drawings themselves would suggest that the travelers probably spent three nights at Salisbury, one night at Southampton, five or six nights at Lymington, a night at Cowes, and two nights at Portsmouth.

Much more problematic than the route and duration of the trip, but also much more fun as a puzzle, is the question of just when the journey took place. In the Capron sale catalogue the date suggested is 1783 or 1784. Grego, however, thought the tour was made in 1782, specifically to view the wreck of the *Royal George*, which had foundered at Spithead on August 29 of that year. Rowlandson does include a drawing of the wreck (No. 66), so unquestionably the journey took place after August 1782. But how soon after is another matter, as the wreck remained visible for many years. Fortunately we also have a *terminus ante quem* for the series. There are many details in the drawings, inconclusive when considered individually but very persuasive collectively, establishing with reasonable certainty that the trip occurred before the end of 1787. Haniford (or Hannaford), whose name appears on the Angel Inn, Lymington, in one of Rowlandson's drawings (No. 36), had ceased to be the proprietor by 1787. The label for the drawing of Pylewell near Lymington (No. 38) gives the owner of the house as Ascanius William Senior. Again, it is known that he sold the house in 1787. The drawing of the Market Place at Salisbury (No. 16) shows the old Bishop's Guildhall that was pulled down about 1788.

It is much more difficult, however, to narrow down the date for the tour within the period 1782 to 1787. There are two references to a ship called the *Hector* (Nos. 61 and 62), which was lying at anchor in Portsmouth Harbour at the time of the trip. This ship was commissioned as a guardship at Spithead in 1783, and it seems very unlikely that Rowlandson could have been aboard her at Portsmouth prior to that date. The *Hector* remained at Spithead for about ten years. Rowlandson also leaves us a drawing of Mrs. Beeston's sea baths at Lymington (No. 32), and from the *Hampshire Chronicle* of May 26, 1783, one would gather that Mrs. Beeston was just at that time taking over the management of the establishment after the death of her husband. The fact that in 1786 Wigstead exhibited at the academy a "View near Freshwater in the Isle of Wight with Smugglers Landing Their Cargo" implies that the trip had taken place by then. Furthermore, as the tour was clearly a summertime excursion and the exhibition opened in May, the expedition from which the drawing was derived probably took place no later than the summer of 1785.

Much more specific evidence concerning date is suggested by the balloon ascent being watched by Rowlandson and his friends at Pylewell (No. 38). As far as is known, Rowlandson could not have witnessed a manned balloon flight prior to September 1784, when Vincenzo Lunardi made his first ascent in England. It is not clear at once from Rowlandson's drawing whether or not he means to suggest a manned balloon, but the shape of the balloon and the fact that the spectators are waving imply that he does. There is no record of any balloon ascent at or near Lymington, and one would hardly expect any experiments so close to the sea. But Jean Pierre Blanchard on his well-known flight from Chelsea on October 16, 1784, landed near Romsey, which is about fifteen miles from Pylewell. It is just possible, though not (it must be admitted) entirely probable, that Rowlandson could have seen Blanchard's balloon from Pylewell. Of course Rowlandson here, as elsewhere, may be indulging in artistic license. But even the idea of such a drawing is most unlikely prior to September 1784, although very probable indeed during that and the following month.

There is one further scrap of tenuous evidence that favors September-October 1784 as the date for the trip. On the back of the drawing labeled "Buying Leather Breeches—Previous to Our Journey" (No. 2) there is an unusually long inscription. This, like the rest of the writing on the backs, can be read only partially and with difficulty. It appears to run as follows: "Mimento 7th Septr sorely troubled with Gripes Windy Cholic & was obliged to stop frequently on my way to Kensington —the heat past bearing dipt in the Serpentine . . . ." The inscription continues for two lines, the only clearly legible words being "the Art of Swimming." The comment obviously does not refer to an episode on the journey itself. As it appears on the back of a drawing depicting early preparations for the trip, one may be justified in concluding that it precedes the journey, probably by several days. There are two details in the inscription that are of particular interest in connection with the date of the tour. Naming the month, September, gives strong confirmation to the suggestion that the trip took place in the early autumn. The reference to heat fits well with what we know of the weather in September 1784. According to the *Gentleman's Magazine*, early September was unusually warm in 1784, the noonday temperature being in the high seventies from the sixth through the twelfth of the month. The temperature on the seventh was seventy-six, hardly "past bearing," yet warm enough for a dip.[13] The corresponding day for 1783, '85, '86, and '87 was appreciably cooler in each instance.

Although the evidence is far from conclusive, there would thus appear to be considerable support favoring late September and early October 1784 as the most likely date for the tour. One hopes that some sharp-eyed antiquarian may yet spot something specific in one of the drawings that will definitely fix the date. On this score, however, it is always necessary to keep in mind that Rowlandson was not a photographer. He occasionally treats detail with considerable license, and it would be

[13] *Gentleman's Magazine*, LV, Pt. 2 (1785), 578.

silly to expect absolute precision from him in the delineation of buildings and landscapes.

The whole problem of the accuracy of individual drawings and the identification of places represented is best left to the notes on each item. In general, however, Rowlandson is fairly reliable, and it is still possible in many instances to locate the spot from which he made a drawing. In those cases where a label appears to be incorrect the fault may lie with the unknown person who mounted the drawings and printed the captions. But one suspects the eighteenth-century traveler would probably have the same sort of difficulty in labeling each of his sketches that the twentieth-century tourist has in remembering where he took each of his photographs. As the final water colors were certainly not worked up on the spot, it would be rather remarkable if Rowlandson, when returning to the sketches, didn't make a single slip in identifying the approximately seventy drawings he made on the trip.

In view of the fact that the sketchbook to which the drawings must originally have belonged has been dismembered and the sketches reshuffled, it is inevitable that one should wonder whether or not the set is now complete. This is a tantalizing problem that does not resolve itself definitely. There appear to have been sixty-seven drawings in the Capron sale; there are now sixty-eight drawings in the set at the Huntington Library. Grego does not make clear in his account whether he is describing actual drawings or merely things he thought the travelers would have seen, so one does not get a definite total from his article. But he does refer specifically to a drawing of Stonehenge. This is not now with the others but may be identified with reasonable certainty as a sketch in the Salisbury, South Wilts and Blackmore Museum. Otherwise Grego's account tallies closely with the drawings at present in the set; and certainly the thirty-seven drawings he illustrates are all now at the Huntington Library. Evidently, then, at least one drawing has been extracted, and (if the count in the Capron sale is accurate) it appears possible that two may have been added.

There are, of course, many other Rowlandson drawings extant with subjects related to this early tour. Some of these may have been derived from the Huntington drawings; some doubtless date from later visits to the same region. Fortunately they are usually different enough in style or physical dimensions to indicate at once that they do not come from the same series.[14] The available evidence implies that the drawings for the

[14]The following drawings, because of physical size and subject matter, may have some relation to the 1784 tour, but in no instance can a definite connection be established:

"Hurst Stokes, Newport River," 4⅝ x 18½ in. Coke sale, Sotheby's, July 21, 1931, Lot 110.

"Newport, High Street, Isle of Wight," 5⅝ x 18½ in. V. P. Sabin,

tour have survived substantially intact, and we need not expect to find any quantity of sketches that would fill in the gaps. Yet one is reluctant to stifle the lingering hope that the journal Wigstead probably wrote to accompany the drawings may still turn up.

Apart from the interesting circumstances surrounding the creation of the series, the drawings themselves are likely to appeal to the spectator in two ways: as fascinating and highly entertaining visual documents concerning life in late eighteenth-century England and as superb examples of line drawing. Rowlandson's position as probably the foremost visual chronicler of the manners and pastimes of his contemporaries has long been recognized, but he is seldom in a more genial and communicative mood than in these early sketches. There is here none of the gross caricature that is often so disturbing, especially in his later work. The primary intention of the drawings was simply to record a journey: humor comes by the way and enters with a nimbler foot and lighter touch than in the more blatantly funny caricatures. Nearly every drawing contains some observation or circumstance that contributes to our understanding of the period. We learn, for instance, about the inside of a man-of-war, the difficulties of putting on leather breeches, the method of making salt, of dealing with captured pirate vessels, of shipping cattle, of dispensing tips. The list could be prolonged indefinitely, for the drawings are almost inexhaustible from this point of view. The more one asks, the more one discovers about the period. We do not, of course, learn much about the great events and major personalities; these we can read about elsewhere. Rowlandson's concern is precisely with those minor circumstances of day-to-day living that are too trivial for the historian but invaluable for revitalizing a particular segment of the past in our imaginations. There is no need to write at length about this facet of the drawings; they speak much more eloquently for themselves.

The approach to the drawings on an art-historical level raises interesting questions concerning Rowlandson's style and chronology. The presence of nearly seventy drawings by Rowlandson that may with reasonable confidence be assigned to a date early in his career provides a unique opportunity for the investigation of the elements of his early style and his technical procedure.

A Catalogue of Watercolour Drawings by Thomas Rowlandson (an exhibition at Frank T. Sabin's galleries, London, 1933), No. 46.

"Steep Hill, near Ventnor, Isle of Wight," 5⅜ x 18 3/16 in. Ibid., No. 68.

Two other drawings have been associated with the 1784 set: "Rowlandson and Wigstead Starting on a Trip" (*Illustrated London News*, Sept. 12, 1936, p. 452); "Rowlandson and Wigstead at the Golden Cross Inn" (Sir Edmund Bacon, Raveningham Hall, Norwich). However, both drawings are too large to belong in the 1784 sketchbook, and they must be associated with one of the other journeys the two men took together.

Although the general nature of Rowlandson's artistic personality is not difficult to discern or define, the more detailed chronicle of his development is a notoriously vexed problem. He did not undergo any profound change of outlook during the half century of his active career, and consequently the differences between his early and late work are not very pronounced. But it is difficult to see even these differences clearly because of the scarcity of firmly dated drawings and the great quantity of repetitions made by Rowlandson and his assistants, especially in the latter part of his life. Even when there is a date in Rowlandson's hand on one of his drawings, we cannot be sure that it gives the actual time of execution. It appears probable that Rowlandson signed and dated many of his drawings long after he drew them. Paul Oppé mentions seeing dates in Rowlandson's hand on paper bearing a later watermark.[15] The problem is further complicated by the fact that we are still very inadequately informed about Rowlandson's assistants, imitators, and copyists. Differences we interpret as stylistic developments may in some instances simply represent the intervention of another hand.

All these factors mean that this early set of drawings, apart from its intrinsic interest, is of great importance to students. For instance, Rowlandson's technical procedure at the beginning of his career can here be studied in considerable detail. It is clear that the drawings all started as outline pencil sketches. Remnants of pencil work are still visible on most of them and are particularly obvious in the landscapes. The next stage was the addition of color. At this period in Rowlandson's career the color is a light, uniform, water-color wash. There is practically no gradation of color within the washes, and no attempt to suggest mass and solidity of elements through modulation in color. In the landscapes, however, the color tends to be stronger, and in one or two instances different hues are run together. The third step was the application, on top of the color, of gray washes. These washes are used to create the shadows and develop the sense of mass in objects. Frequently they reinforce the contours of trees or hills and take on the character of broad, soft lines.

The final phase in the development of the drawing involved the use of pen. It is, of course, the penwork that is the most personal, flexible, and artistically the most significant feature of the drawings. The penwork is used for figures and also for objects that because of their closeness to the spectator, or because of the precision with which Rowlandson wishes to present them, cannot be satisfactorily delineated in wash. In this series of draw-

[15] *Thomas Rowlandson: His Drawings and Water-colours* (London, 1923), pp. 5-6. A dated drawing on paper with a later watermark is in the Metropolitan Museum.

ings the line is blackish brown and applied with a pen that has the virtuosity of a fine calligrapher's brush. At times the line is simply a contour defining the edge of an object; on other occasions it can ebb and swell in a most eloquent fashion to suggest the solidity and whole spatial existence of a figure. The tailpiece (No. 14) is from this standpoint one of Rowlandson's most brilliant performances. The penwork, although obviously laid down with great vigor and freedom, is extraordinarily successful not only in delineating the contours of the horses but also in giving them solidity and direction of movement. And simply as lines, regardless of what they represent, they have all the appeal of the finest calligraphy.

Drawings of this type are the work not only of a highly talented artist, but also of one who has spent much time in the acquisition of such ease and facility of execution. The steps by which Rowlandson developed his talent to the level at which we find it in this early series remain something of a mystery. The number of known drawings from his hand that may be dated with certainty prior to 1784 is pitifully small and provides hardly any framework for conjecture concerning his development as an artist. Two drawings exist that may with reasonable conviction be assigned to the mid-1770's.[16] But these, although entertaining caricatures, are hardly more than juvenilia and certainly do not prepare us for the next group of drawings we encounter a decade later, all at just about the time of the tour with which we are concerned. Clearly it was during this interval that Rowlandson's artistic personality matured. It is puzzling that so few of the considerable number of drawings he must have produced during those ten years have survived and been identified.

In its general character there is nothing particularly original in Rowlandson's art and little for which there is not a parallel in the work of older contemporaries in England. He did not invent either a new genre or a new style. His humorous, anecdotal type of subject matter is widespread through mid-eighteenth-century British and European painting. Hogarth comes to mind at once as a predecessor, although the serious satiric intent running through much of his art sets him apart from Rowlandson, who was generally content simply to observe and poke fun without pointing a moral. Closer in spirit to Rowlandson (and also closer in date) is a man like Parisian-trained James de Loutherbourg, whose "A Midsummer Afternoon with a Methodist Preacher" (exhibited at the Royal Academy in 1777) is very similar in outlook to the slightly later work of his younger con-

[16]"School of Eloquence," in the Royal Library, Windsor (reproduced in Oppé, *Thomas Rowlandson: His Drawings and Water-colours*, Pl. 1); "A Bench of Artists Sketched at the Royal Academy in the Year 1776," Oppé collection (reproduced in Hayes, Pl. 23A).

temporary (Fig. 1). The relationship between this painting and the work of Rowlandson has not gone undetected,[17] but unfortunately we know too little about the careers of Rowlandson and De Loutherbourg in the mid-1770's to draw any definite conclusions about the influence one may have had on the other. The general circumstances imply clearly, however, that if there was any connection, it was Rowlandson who was the beneficiary. Certainly we have nothing from him before the early 1780's that could possibly have served as a model for De Loutherbourg. On the other hand, a painting such as "A Midsummer Afternoon with a Methodist Preacher" could provide at least the principal bridge necessary to get from the two known Rowlandson drawings of the mid-1770's to the first great exhibition pieces of 1784. It is not only in the treatment of individual figures but also in the whole organization of the composition that one senses a kinship between, for instance, "The Serpentine River" and the work of De Loutherbourg. The humorous genre picture was only one of the strings on De Loutherbourg's fiddle—and a string on which he didn't choose to play very often. If Rowlandson did take a hint from De Loutherbourg, he developed it far beyond anything the older man attempted. Nevertheless, De Loutherbourg does anticipate closely the outlook embodied in Rowlandson's first important drawings.

Rowlandson's basic technique, the tinted drawing, is shared by so many of his contemporaries that the question of influences becomes highly academic. Once again De Loutherbourg and also Julius Caesar Ibbetson and Francis Wheatley (to mention only a few) adopt a similar procedure. A specific connection of some interest exists between Rowlandson and Wheatley. In the mid-1780's Rowlandson engraved a series of plates called "Imitations of Modern Drawings." It has been generally assumed, in accordance with the meaning we now attach to "imitation," that the sources for the plates were drawings of Rowlandson's own creation in the manners of the various artists concerned. However, it may well be that Rowlandson intended the word to be understood in the more normal eighteenth-century sense, which is similar in meaning to our modern "reproduction." In any event, what may be the original of one of Rowlandson's "imitations" of Wheatley is now in the Huntington collection (Fig. 2). The drawing, certainly by Wheatley himself, is the reverse of Rowlandson's print; the drawing is dated 1782, and the print, 1786.[18] The technical procedure adopted by Wheatley is precisely that used by Rowlandson in the 1784 tour. And yet, in

[17]Falk, pp. 184-185; Ellis K. Waterhouse, *Painting in Britain 1530 to 1790* (Baltimore, 1953), p. 234.

[18]A repetition of the Wheatley drawing, also dated 1782, is in the collection of Alan D. Pilkington.

spite of all the similarities, it is the difference between the Wheatley drawing and one by Rowlandson that is really important. The vitality and virtuosity of Rowlandson's penwork is nowhere apparent in the other drawing. Wheatley's line is simply outline, nothing more.

In discussing parallels to and possible sources for Rowlandson's early style, there is yet one further problem that should be raised, even if it must subsequently be left floating in the air. Rowlandson's companion on the journey, Henry Wigstead, was also a draftsman, although in this capacity he is a very elusive figure. At the Royal Academy exhibition of 1785 he was accused by the critic writing for the *St. James's Chronicle* of displaying as his own, drawings that were patently the work of Rowlandson. "These humorous and excellent drawings," says the critic of Wigstead's 1785 exhibits, "we make no doubt to be the production of Mr. Rowlandson; and we wonder anyone should exhibit them as his own whose abilities are known to be unequal to the invention or execution of such drawings. And what shall we say of the penetration of the Rulers of the Academy who could not see in them the hand of Rowlandson?"[19] Modifying the impression created by this statement is the obituary notice in the *Gentleman's Magazine*, which indicates clearly that Wigstead had a considerable reputation as a caricaturist in his own right. But there are no absolutely certain drawings from his hand. The prints bearing his name are customarily considered to have been executed by Rowlandson after Wigstead's suggestions, a relationship given considerable support by the comments in the *St. James's Chronicle*.[20] And yet it is quite possible we are doing Wigstead a serious injustice in this matter.

The earliest scrap of visual material associated with Rowlandson is a print of 1774 bearing the initials "H. W." Grego assumes the execution is by Rowlandson from an idea suggested by Wigstead, and he is probably correct.[21] But it is surely distinctly interesting that Wigstead should be taking the credit at Rowlandson's debut, ten years before the younger man emerges clearly as an artist in his own right.

There is a drawing in the Huntington collection that offers further ground for speculation concerning the artistic relation between the two men. It is a political caricature of the Younger Pitt and relates to the Regency Crisis of late 1788 and early 1789 (Fig. 3). The drawing is signed "H. Wigstead invent.," and the signature is

[19]Quoted in William T. Whitley, *Artists and Their Friends in England 1700-1799* (London, 1928), II, 396-397.

[20]This interpretation, given by Grego to prints apparently by Rowlandson that bear Wigstead's name or initials, is followed by M. D. George in *Catalogue of Political and Personal Satires* (London, 1938), Vol. VI.

[21]Grego, *Rowlandson the Caricaturist*, I, 96-97.

The National Gallery of Canada

FIG. 1. JAMES DE LOUTHERBOURG. A MIDSUMMER AFTERNOON WITH A METHODIST PREACHER.

FIG. 2. FRANCIS WHEATLEY. PALMERSTON FAIR.

authentic.[22] The drawing is extraordinarily close in style to Rowlandson. Portions of it in isolation (the portrait of Mrs. Schwellenberg and the skirt of Queen Charlotte) would certainly pass as his work. But the principal figures, the Younger Pitt and the petitioners, have a flat, spindly quality that is outside Rowlandson's normal style. The fact that in signing the drawing Wigstead used the formula "invent." rather than "delin." still leaves open the possibility that Rowlandson may have had a part in the execution. Yet the visual evidence implies that another hand is also involved. If, as would appear to be the case, this drawing is actually by Wigstead, then his style is even closer to that of Rowlandson than the known connections between the two men would suggest; and the connoisseurship problem in distinguishing between their two hands will be an exacting one. The most interesting part of the connection is the common use of a free, sketchy type of pen line, something that is much rarer in the work of Rowlandson's contemporaries than the other components of his style. Of course, in this supposed Wigstead drawing the line has little of the descriptive power and calligraphic elegance of Rowlandson's. One is inclined to assume that the influence must have moved from the more to the less gifted man. And yet, in the absence of definite information about Wigstead's artistic personality, one cannot immediately dismiss the possibility that Rowlandson may have seen something he could turn to his own advantage in the work of his older friend.

Curiously enough, this brilliant early phase of Rowlandson's technique is not developed or even consistently maintained in his later work. Insofar as one is able to generalize at all, it appears that Rowlandson's penwork becomes less versatile as his career develops. The line is more and more concerned with simple definition of contour. The modeling and construction of the forms are performed more by color. The line also loses much of its calligraphic elegance. At the extreme end of the scale is a drawing such as "The Band" on paper watermarked 1826 (one year before the artist's death), in which the penwork forms a fine outline of absolute uniformity (Fig. 4). But this small drawing also raises the whole question of copies, replicas, and variants that Rowlandson and others made of his subjects. There is another version of this drawing in the Huntington collection, and it is clear from direct comparison that one is traced from the other, or both from a common source. The same subject appeared in reverse, and apparently larger in scale, at a Sotheby sale on November 18, 1953.

That Rowlandson was already making repetitions of his drawings early in his career is clear from the evidence on the backs of many sketches made during his

[22]Authentic Wigstead signatures may be found in the Kensington rate books for 1798 and 1799, when he was justice of the peace.

1784 tour. One is greatly handicapped by being unable to examine the backs directly, but there are fully developed drawings on many of them. Most of these have exact counterparts elsewhere in the series. They are almost certainly the original drafts, which Rowlandson repeated to avoid losing the design when the drawings were mounted and the double-sheet paste-ups were made. The repetitions are certainly by Rowlandson himself, although there are some very minor stylistic differences suggesting a lapse of time between the first and second drafts. The most interesting fact, however, is that the outlines of the two are so close there can be little doubt that the second draft at least started as a direct tracing from the first (see illus. facing No. 51).

The collection of other Rowlandson material in the Huntington Library is sufficiently large that there are many repetitions, and we can study the various ways employed by the artist and his assistants to reproduce his drawings. Besides tracing and free variants, he apparently resorted occasionally to various types of counterproofing and often transposed groups or single figures from one subject to another.[23] In nearly all these instances the initial line obtained by tracing or counterproofing is subsequently reinforced by pen. Unfortunately we are not now, nor are we ever likely to be, in possession of information that will enable us to determine which of these later repetitions are actually by Rowlandson. And yet the problem is probably less important than it may seem at first. The mere fact that he is known to have made repetitions himself is the significant consideration. The versatile, flexible, and highly personal penwork one finds in the drawings from the 1780's cannot be easily traced. It does not even lend itself readily to engraving, a medium that occupied more and more of Rowlandson's time as his career progressed. Clearly a uniform contour line was more serviceable for duplication (by tracing, counterproofing, or engraving) than the type of line one encounters in Rowlandson's early drawings. This in itself may be sufficient to account for the modification in the artist's penwork. But Rowlandson was also following the general trend of the times. His contemporaries, men like John Flaxman, Thomas Stothard, and William Blake, all developed a willowy type of linearism.

Fortunately, however, there is no need to dwell at length on the problems and vicissitudes of Rowlandson's later career. Our concern is with one of his most brilliant youthful productions. If it is a rather sad fact that Rowlandson seldom again attained this level of excellence,

[23]There are in particular two incomplete drawings in the Huntington collection (132504, Nos. 70 and 107) in which the initial outlines have clearly been obtained by some sort of counterproofing process. This evidence tends to confirm the description of Rowlandson's methods of duplication given in *Notes and Queries*, Ser. 4, IV (1869), 89. Most of the duplications, however, are straight tracings or free variants.

FIG. 3. HENRY WIGSTEAD. THE PRIVATE SECRETARY BESTOWING ALMS.

FIG. 4. THOMAS ROWLANDSON. THE BAND.

that consideration surely need not interfere with our enjoyment of the drawings themselves. As records of the time, as humorous anecdotes, as pen and wash sketches, they could hardly be better, and they constitute one of the most impressive documents we have in support of the great reputation Rowlandson enjoyed with his contemporaries.

A NOTE ON BIBLIOGRAPHY

ALTHOUGH Rowlandson is one of the most popular of British artists, and brief accounts of his work appear in countless books, he has not in fact been the object of much serious scholarship. Our chief source of biographical information about him is the obituary notice printed in the *Gentleman's Magazine*, XCVII, Pt. 1 (1827), pp. 564-565. This account cannot be relied on for all details, but there seems no reason to doubt that the picture it presents of the artist is accurate in general outline. It is curious that Rowlandson, who was certainly not an obscure artist in his own day, does not figure more prominently in the memoirs of his contemporaries. W. H. Pyne (writing under the name of Ephraim Hardcastle) mentions him in *Wine and Walnuts* (London, 1824), II, 323-327, and again in *Somerset House Gazette* (London, 1824), II, 222, 347, and 360. Rowlandson's friend Henry Angelo also talks about the artist in *Reminiscences* (London, 1828-1830). But there is little else from his contemporaries. An interesting exchange concerning the artist sprang up in *Notes and Queries*, Ser. 4, Vol. IV (1869). One contributor, identified only as W. P., gives a fascinating account of Rowlandson's method of duplicating drawings by counterproofing (see Introduction, p. 21 and n. 23).

Of the later books on Rowlandson probably the most important is the vast, rambling, two-volume work by Joseph Grego, *Rowlandson the Caricaturist* (London, 1880). The best general account of his art remains that by A. Paul Oppé, *Thomas Rowlandson: His Drawings and Water-colours* (London, 1923). A more recent publication, of particular interest for new light it sheds on Rowlandson's biography and family background, is by Bernard Falk, *Thomas Rowlandson: His Life and Art* (London, [1949]). Other general books on the artist include: F. Gordon Roe, *Rowlandson: The Life and Art of a British Genius* (Leigh-on-Sea, England, 1947); Adrian Bury, *Rowlandson Drawings* (London, 1949); and Arthur W. Heintzelman, *The Watercolor Drawings of Thomas Rowlandson from the Albert H. Wiggin Collection in the Boston Public Library* (New York, 1947). Two more specialized studies of considerable interest are: Richard M. Baum, "A Rowlandson Chronology," *Art Bulletin*, XX (1938), 237-250; and Edward C. J. Wolf, *Rowlandson and His Illustrations of Eighteenth Century English Literature* (Copenhagen, 1945).

There have been numerous exhibitions devoted to Rowlandson, and several of the catalogues retain permanent scholarly interest. An important exhibition of books illustrated by Rowlandson was held at the Grolier Club, New York, November 2 to 23, 1916. There have been several exhibitions of Rowlandson drawings at the galleries of Frank T. Sabin (London), including a particularly impressive one in 1933. Much of the splendid collection of Rowlandson drawings formerly belonging to Gilbert Davis, Esq., was exhibited at the Arts Council, London, 1950. A succinct and scholarly catalogue by John Hayes of the Rowlandson drawings in the London Museum was issued in 1960.

A TOUR IN A POST CHAISE

1. MR. ROWLANDSON HIRING THE FIRST POST-CHAISE

2. BUYING LEATHER BREECHES—PREVIOUS TO OUR JOURNEY

3. TRUNK SHOP—MR. WIGSTEAD BARGAINING

4. MYSELF AT DINNER

5. MR. ROWLANDSON'S OLD HOUSEKEEPER CALLING HIM UP ON THE MORNING WE SET OFF

6. MR. WIGSTEAD TAKING LEAVE OF HIS HOME AND FAMILY—THE START

7. CHAISE AT THE DOOR, SETTING OUT FROM ROWLANDSON'S HOUSE IN WARDOUR STREET

8. THE FIRST STAGE FROM LONDON—"KING'S HEAD INN YARD," HOUNSLOW, ARRIVED AT 7 O'CLOCK

9. BREAKFAST AT EGHAM

10. THE WHITE HART INN, BAGSHOT

11. THE "SPREAD EAGLE" AT HOOK

12. THE DELAY—OR ACCIDENT, AT POPHAM LANE—1 O'CLOCK

13. THE CONTEST FOR PRECEDENCE OVER THE DOWNS BETWEEN STOCKBRIDGE AND SALISBURY

14. HEAD AND TAIL-PIECE—VIEW (FRONT) FROM POST-CHAISE

15. COFFEE HOUSE IN SALISBURY MARKET PLACE

16. SALISBURY MARKET PLACE

17. [A MONUMENT IN SALISBURY CATHEDRAL]

18. [THE YARD OF AN INN]

19. STONEHENGE

20. THE "GRAND ROOM" IN WILTON HOUSE, NEAR SALISBURY, THE SEAT OF THE EARL OF PEMBROKE

21. THE DEPARTURE FROM THE "WHITE HART," SALISBURY

22. [ARRIVAL AT AN INN]

23. THE BAR, SOUTHAMPTON

24. VIEW IN SOUTHAMPTON RIVER

25. OUR ARRIVAL AT THE "COACH & HORSES" SOUTHAMPTON; THE CHAISE WAITING TO CARRY US TO LYMINGTON

26. THE CHURCH, THE "CROWN INN," AND THE DUKE OF GLOUCESTER'S STABLES AT LYNDHURST, IN THE NEW FOREST, HAMPSHIRE

27. [A BARBER'S SHOP]

28. FIRST INTERVIEW WITH TWO FEMALE FRIENDS ON OUR ARRIVAL AT LYMINGTON

29. [THE YARD OF THE ANGEL INN, LYMINGTON]

30. FRUIT SHOP AT LYMINGTON—MR. WIGSTEAD MAKING FRIENDS

31. INSIDE OF A SALTERN AT LYMINGTON, WITH THE MANNER OF MAKING SALT

32. MRS. BEESTON'S BATHS AT LYMINGTON

33. A COTTAGE AT LYMINGTON

34. FIRST INTERVIEW WITH A FRIEND AT LYMINGTON

35. THE LANDLORD WHERE WE LODGED AT LYMINGTON COMPLAINING OF HIS MISFORTUNES

36. THE ANGEL INN AT LYMINGTON

37. KITCHEN AT THE INN AT LYMINGTON, ON ROAD TO PILESWELL

38. PILESWELL, NEAR LYMINGTON IN HAMPSHIRE—THE SEAT OF ASCANIUS WILLIAM SENIOR, ESQ[RE]

39. THE OLD WHISKEY, LYMINGTON

40. ROWLANDSON TALKING WITH A LADY, OUTSIDE THE "ANGEL" LYMINGTON

41. "PITT'S DEEP," NEAR HURST CASTLE, A LITTLE ALE HOUSE FAMOUS FOR SELLING GOOD BRANDY

42. SHIPPING OXEN ON BOARD THE ISLE OF WIGHT PACKET

43. WIGSTEAD'S PARTING INTERVIEW WITH HIS LYMINGTON FRIEND

44. LYMINGTON QUAY, WITH THE METHOD OF SHIPPING CATTLE FOR THE ISLE OF WIGHT

A MAP OF SOUTHERN HAMPSHIRE AND THE ISLE OF WIGHT, FROM [JOHN] *Cary's New and Correct English Atlas* (London, 1787)

45. THE PRETTY HOSTESS, AND ROWLANDSON—WITH THE EXTRAVAGANT BILL, AND WIGSTEAD

46. LYMINGTON RIVER, NEAR THE QUAY—GOING ON BOARD THE VESSEL TO CARRY US TO THE ISLE OF WIGHT

47. LYMINGTON TO THE NEEDLES—ON BOARD THE PACKET

48. THE QUARTER-DECK OF THE VESSEL WHICH CARRIED US TO THE NEEDLES—THE WIND BLOWING HARD

49. SIX MILES FROM YARMOUTH—ALUM BAY

50. PART OF THE ROCKS IN ALUM BAY

PRELIMINARY DRAWING FOR NO. 47, ON THE VERSO OF NO. 55,
PHOTOGRAPHED THROUGH THE MOUNT WITH SPECIAL LIGHT

51. THE NEEDLE ROCKS, FROM THE SEA

52. THE NEEDLE ROCKS

53. ST. CHRISTOPHER'S ROCK

54. [THE WESTERN END OF THE ISLE OF WIGHT FROM THE SOLENT]

55. [THE ISLE OF WIGHT AS SEEN FROM THE BLUFFS ABOVE THE NEEDLES]

56. A GENERAL VIEW OF THE ISLE OF WIGHT

57. COWES HARBOUR IN THE ISLE OF WIGHT

58. COWES HARBOUR IN THE ISLE OF WIGHT

59. THE BOAT WHICH WE HIRED FROM COWES TO PORTSMOUTH

60. AT SUPPER IN PORTSMOUTH ON OUR ARRIVAL FROM COWES; ALL VERY MUCH FATIGUED

61. GOING ON BOARD THE "HECTOR," OF 74 GUNS, LYING IN PORTSMOUTH HARBOUR

62. MIDDLE DECK OF THE "HECTOR," MAN-OF-WAR

A PHOTOGRAPH TAKEN AT HOOK, HAMPSHIRE, IN SEPTEMBER 1961
OF THE BUILDING DRAWN BY ROWLANDSON IN NO. 11

63. THE MANNER OF WORKING THE GUNS ON BOARD A SHIP IN TIME OF ACTION

Custom House Corner

64. CUSTOM HOUSE CORNER, PORTSMOUTH, WITH A SMUGGLING VESSEL CUT IN TWO

SLOP SHOP

65. PORTSMOUTH POINT, WITH A DISTANT VIEW OF GOSPORT

66. SPITHEAD, WITH THE EXACT SITUATION AND APPEARANCE OF THE "ROYAL GEORGE," WRECKED AUGUST 29, 1782

67. COTTAGES, FARNHAM, SURREY

68. AN EARTHENWARE SHOP AT FARNHAM, SURREY

69. ["THE TUMBLE-DOWN-DICK"]

NOTES ON THE ILLUSTRATIONS

Rowlandson complicated the job of reproducing the drawings by his practice of occasionally gluing together two pages of his sketchbook in order to make a double-sized sheet. The only practicable way to reproduce these double drawings in proper sequence without reducing the scale was to place their separate halves on either side of an opening. This arrangement in turn left three pages blank in the latter part of the book. These pages have been used to illustrate other material related to the tour: facing No. 45, a map of southern Hampshire and the Isle of Wight; facing No. 51, a photograph taken with the aid of special light to reveal a drawing on the verso of a sheet pasted to a mount; facing No. 63, a modern photograph of one of the sites drawn by Rowlandson.

1. MR. ROWLANDSON HIRING THE FIRST POST-CHAISE*

4 7/8 x 7 7/8 in.

A sign in the background reads "Neat Post Chaises Saddle Horses / Hearses Glass Coaches / Phaetons Whiskeys Gigs / to lett. Horses stand at / Livery. . . ."

2. BUYING LEATHER BREECHES – PREVIOUS TO OUR JOURNEY

4 15/16 x 7 7/8 in.

VERSO: *Inscribed, but only partially decipherable, "Mimento 7th Septr sorely troubled with Gripes Windy Cholic & was obliged to stop frequently on my way to Kensington—the heat past bearing dipt in the Serpentine in my . . . home . . . practise not . . . the Art of Swimming."*

A sign on the wall reads "Fitch Breeches maker to his Higness [sic] the Pr . . . ." *The Universal British Directory of Trade and Commerce* (London, 1790), p. 145, lists John Fitch, Breeches-maker and Glover, 195 Piccadilly. Fitch's name does not appear in earlier directories of London tradesmen, but as the earlier directories are not nearly so exhaustive as the one of 1790, the absence of his name does not necessarily mean that he was not in business.

3. TRUNK SHOP – MR. WIGSTEAD BARGAINING

5 x 7 3/4 in.

INSCRIBED: *"Trunk Shop—Mr. W. bargaining."*

VERSO: *A three-line inscription, of which the only decipherable words are ". . . having cast an eye upon our . . . her recommendation . . . ."*

A sign in the background reads "Drivenn[?] Trunk Maker." *The Universal British Directory of Trade and Commerce* (London, 1790), p. 131, lists Messrs. Drivers, Trunkmakers, 70 Charing Cross and 10 Strand.

*Unless placed in brackets, the titles given are those printed on the mounts. See Introduction, pp. 7-8.

4. MYSELF AT DINNER

5 x 7 13/16 in.

Numbered in pencil in lower right corner "13."

This drawing is stylistically isolated from the rest of the series. The subject also does not seem to have much connection with the preparations for the journey. Probably the drawing was not originally part of the set.

5. MR. ROWLANDSON'S OLD HOUSEKEEPER CALLING HIM UP ON THE MORNING WE SET OFF

5 x 7 13/16 in.

INSCRIBED: *"Sir. Sir. Sir. its past 4 O'Clock."*

6. MR. WIGSTEAD TAKING LEAVE OF HIS HOME AND FAMILY – THE START

5 x 7 7/8 in.

INSCRIBED: *"You may expect to see me again Sunday Sennight."*

As far as is known, Wigstead was at this time living in Gerrard Street, Soho, within a few blocks of Rowlandson's residence in Wardour Street.

7. CHAISE AT THE DOOR, SETTING OUT FROM ROWLANDSON'S HOUSE IN WARDOUR STREET

4 15/16 x 7 3/4 in.

INSCRIBED: *"Chaise at the Door."*

Rowlandson lived at 103 Wardour Street, Soho, from 1777 through 1786.

8. THE FIRST STAGE FROM LONDON – "KING'S HEAD INN YARD," HOUNSLOW, ARRIVED AT 7 O'CLOCK

4 15/16 x 7 7/8 in.

INSCRIBED: "King's Head Inn Yard. Hounslow arrived at 7 O Clock–."

VERSO: *Inscribed, only partially decipherable, "A curious piece of French poetry*

> *F . . . moi de . . . , F . . . de toute que vois nous sommes des . . . nous faire . . . ."*

John Cary's *New Itinerary* (London, 1798) records the King's Head as one of the principal coaching inns at Hounslow, p. 39.

9. BREAKFAST AT EGHAM

4 15/16 x 7 1/2 in.

INSCRIBED: *"Please your Honours Remember your Post Boy."*

VERSO: *An undecipherable inscription.*

10. THE WHITE HART INN, BAGSHOT

4⅞ x 7¾ in.

VERSO: *An undecipherable inscription.*

John Cary's *New Itinerary* (London, 1798) records the White Hart as a coaching inn at Bagshot, p. 39.

11. THE "SPREAD EAGLE" AT HOOK

5 x 8 in.

INSCRIBED: *"Hook A Village 43 Miles from London. stopt at the Spread Eagle."*

An inn, which certainly appears to be the one drawn by Rowlandson, still stands, and is now called the White Hart. According to local tradition it was previously called the Spread Eagle. See illustration facing No. 63.

12. THE DELAY – OR ACCIDENT, AT POPHAM LANE – 1 O'CLOCK

5 x 8 in.

INSCRIBED: *"The Delay or Accident Popham Lane 1 O Clock."*
VERSO: *A drawing of a building and an inscription, "Stockbridge arrived with a tolerable appetite at three, dined at the White Hart 68 miles from London."*

13. THE CONTEST FOR PRECEDENCE OVER THE DOWNS BETWEEN STOCKBRIDGE AND SALISBURY

5 x 8 in.

INSCRIBED: *"The Contest."*

14. HEAD AND TAIL-PIECE – VIEW (FRONT) FROM POST-CHAISE

4½ x 7 5/16 in.

Grego mentions this drawing in connection with "The Contest for Precedence over the Downs," where it probably belongs, although (as he also points out) it makes an effective tailpiece.

15. COFFEE HOUSE IN SALISBURY MARKET PLACE

5 x 7⅞ in.

INSCRIBED: *"Coffee House in Market Place at Salisbury."*

VERSO: *First draft of drawing No. 17; inscribed "Buchamp monument in Salisbury . . . ."*

On the table is a newspaper labeled "Morning Chronicle" (printed in London from 1770 to 1862).

The interior represented may be the Parade Coffee House on the Blue Boar Row.

16. SALISBURY MARKET PLACE

4⅞ x 7⅞ in.

INSCRIBED: *"Salisbury – Markett Place."*

VERSO: *Inscribed "... at the White Hart, Salisbury."*

The Council House is shown after the fire of 1780, which destroyed part of the top story. The old Bishop's Guildhall, standing behind, was pulled down about 1788.

17. [A MONUMENT IN SALISBURY CATHEDRAL]

4⅞ x 7 15/16 in.

The caption on the mount reads "Earl Beauchamp's Monument in Salisbury Cathedral." The reference is probably to Bishop Richard Beauchamp's Chantry Chapel, which was built against the south wall of the Lady Chapel in the cathedral. It was demolished by Wyatt in 1789. There were several effigies in the chapel, but it is not now possible to determine which one Rowlandson has drawn. The drawing is probably simply a general recollection.

The first draft of this drawing is on the verso of No. 15.

18. [THE YARD OF AN INN]

5 x 8 in.

VERSO: *A first draft of the left half of No. 19.*

The caption on the mount reads "The Angel Inn Yard, Lymington"; but the Exeter Post Coach (standing in the foreground) did not stop at Lymington. It appears probable that the caption somehow became misplaced from No. 29. The inn represented would have to be somewhere along the Exeter road between London and Salisbury. The innyard of the White Hart, Salisbury, is a likely candidate. The area has now changed considerably, but the general layout is similar. The fact that a drawing of Stonehenge is on the verso further supports Salisbury as the location of the inn.

19. STONEHENGE

4⅞ x 15 9/16 in.

VERSO: *Inscribed "Wilton House, the seat of Earl Pembroke, and a most capital collection of marble antiques and ancient pictures."*

Reproduced by courtesy of the Salisbury, South Wilts and Blackmore Museum, Salisbury.

This drawing, which is now in the Salisbury, South Wilts and Blackmore Museum, clearly belongs to Rowlandson's 1784 tour. It is on the same type of paper, is the same size as the double sheets, and is completely consistent stylistically with the other drawings. Grego refers specifically to a drawing of Stonehenge in his 1891 account. Furthermore, a first draft of the left half of the drawing is on the verso of No. 18.

Very little is known about the previous history of the Salisbury Museum drawing. It entered the museum in 1900 with the collection of Job Edwards, an antiquary of Amesbury, Wilts.

20. THE "GRAND ROOM" IN WILTON HOUSE, NEAR SALISBURY, THE SEAT OF THE EARL OF PEMBROKE

4 13/16 x 7¾ in.

VERSO: *Inscribed, only partially legible, ". . . Romsey 96 miles from . . . . Memorandum Washing Chambermaids, Post boys, hostlers . . . minding the departure . . . difficult to get . . ."*

This is a free recollection of the double cube room at Wilton. Rowlandson is pointing at the large Van Dyck group portrait of the Pembroke family.

The remnants of an inscription trimmed from the drawing remain on the bottom margin.

21. THE DEPARTURE FROM THE "WHITE HART," SALISBURY

5 x 7⅞ in.

INSCRIBED: *"The Departure from White Hart Salisbury."*

VERSO: *Slight sketch and generally undecipherable inscription. The only words that can be read are ". . . little Gibson . . ."*

The drawing shows the inn before the addition of the portico, which now projects in front of the arch. To the left is the Bell and Crown Inn.

22. [ARRIVAL AT AN INN]

4 15/16 x 7 15/16 in.

The caption on the mount reads "The White Hart Inn Yard at Salisbury," but the area represented bears no relation in appearance or general layout to the White Hart Innyard. The drawing may depict the arrival at the Coach and Horses, Southampton. A caption mentioning this event is included incongruously with the label for No. 25.

23. THE BAR, SOUTHAMPTON

5 x 8 in.

The rendering of the Bargate (seen from the north) is certainly not accurate in detail, but there seems no reason to doubt that the drawing is correctly labeled.

For a print showing the gate in 1771 see F. J. C. Hearnshaw et al., *A Short History of Southampton* (Oxford, 1910), frontispiece.

24. VIEW IN SOUTHAMPTON RIVER

5 x 8 in.

VERSO: *Sketch of a rocky bank.*

25. OUR ARRIVAL AT THE "COACH & HORSES" SOUTHAMPTON; THE CHAISE WAITING TO CARRY US TO LYMINGTON

5 x 7 15/16 in.

John Cary's *New Itinerary* (London, 1798) records the Coach and Horses as a coaching inn at Southampton, p. 50.

Apparently two captions have been telescoped. The first part may refer to drawing No. 22.

26. THE CHURCH, THE "CROWN INN," AND THE DUKE OF GLOUCESTER'S STABLES AT LYNDHURST, IN THE NEW FOREST, HAMPSHIRE

4 7/8 x 15 3/4 in.

VERSO LEFT-HAND SHEET: *First draft for drawing No. 27.*

Richard Warner, Jr., *A Companion in a Tour round Lymington* (Southampton, [1789]), p. 42, speaking of the office of Lord Warden of the New Forest, states that it "belong'd formerly (according to Leland,) by right of inheritance, to the Earls of *Arundel*; was the latter part of the last century in the *Bolton* family, has since then been held by the dukes of *Bedford*, and is now fill'd by his Royal Highness the *Duke* of *Glocester*." Both the church and the Crown Inn were rebuilt in the nineteenth century.

John Cary's *New Itinerary* (London, 1798) records The Crown as a coaching inn at Lyndhurst, p. 58.

27. [A BARBER'S SHOP]

5 x 8 in.

The caption for this drawing reads "Barber's Shop, Alresford." Alresford, to the east of Winchester, is not on the route probably used by Rowlandson and Wigstead. Furthermore, as the first draft of this drawing occurs on the back of No. 26, one suspects the building represented was probably somewhere in the New Forest.

28. FIRST INTERVIEW WITH TWO FEMALE FRIENDS ON OUR ARRIVAL AT LYMINGTON

5 x 7 7/8 in.

INSCRIBED IN PENCIL: *"The Rendezvous" [?].*

29. [THE YARD OF THE ANGEL INN, LYMINGTON]

4 15/16 x 16 in.

VERSO LEFT-HAND SHEET: *First draft of drawing No. 34.*

The caption on the mount reads "High Street, Southampton," but this is surely an error. Edward King reproduced the drawing in *Old Times Re-visited in the Borough and Parish of Lymington, Hants.*, 2nd ed. (London and Lymington, 1900), facing p. 260, and there called it the yard of the Angel Inn, Lymington. The area has now changed considerably but is still sufficiently similar to make the identification plausible.

30. FRUIT SHOP AT LYMINGTON—
MR. WIGSTEAD MAKING FRIENDS

4 15/16 x 8 1/16 in.

INSCRIBED VERY LIGHTLY IN PENCIL: *"Fruit Shop."*

31. INSIDE OF A SALTERN AT LYMINGTON, WITH THE MANNER OF MAKING SALT

4 15/16 x 8 in.

INSCRIBED: *"Salt Pans Mode of Making."*

VERSO: *Drawing of a cottage with figures leaning on a fence.*

Richard Warner, Jr., *A Companion in a Tour round Lymington* (Southampton, [1789]), p. 11, comments on Lymington salt: "The superiority of the *Lymington* salt, to that made in any other part throughout the kingdom, (for the purpose of preserving) had for a long series of years, render'd it the most considerable place both for the manufactory and sale of this article; but being of late greatly undersold, by the inhabitants of *Droitwich, Nantwich* etc. (who are enabled by several local advantages, to dispose of it at a much cheaper rate than the Lymington manufacturer) the works have been sometime rapidly on the decline, and are now verging very fast towards annihilation."

32. MRS. BEESTON'S BATHS AT LYMINGTON

4 15/16 x 16 1/8 in.

VERSO: *Sea sketches.*

Richard Warner, Jr., *A Companion in a Tour round Lymington* (Southampton, [1789]), p. 13: "Among the many conveniences *Lymington* enjoys, we must not omit to mention its *bathing houses*. They consist of two sets, one situated at the bottom of the town, and the other at the distance of half a mile from it. They are both well calculated to answer the purposes, for which they were erected. The latter however seem chiefly to be resorted to; and perhaps the superior neatness and convenience of them, assisted by the unwearied assiduity of their proprietor, may have given them a preference not altogether undeserv'd."

Hampshire Chronicle, May 26, 1783: "Mrs. Beeston of Lymington Sea Baths informs frequenters of her late husband's Bathing House that she will exert her utmost abilities to continue the same warmth and salubrity." A similar advertisement was inserted in the *Hampshire Chronicle* by Mrs. Beeston on May 2, 1783. (A James Beeston of Lymington was buried late in November 1782, age 55.)

The first draft of this drawing occurs on the verso of No. 41.

33. A COTTAGE AT LYMINGTON

4 7/8 x 15 11/16 in.

34. FIRST INTERVIEW WITH A FRIEND AT LYMINGTON

4⅝ x 7 15/16 in.

WATERMARK: *J. Whatman (see note to No. 53).*

It is tempting to suppose that the clerical-looking friend who figures in this and drawing No. 43 may be William Gilpin, vicar of Boldre. Lymington lay within the parish of Boldre. The common interest of Wigstead and Gilpin in picturesque travel would provide a bond of friendship. The first draft of this drawing is on the verso of No. 29.

35. THE LANDLORD WHERE WE LODGED AT LYMINGTON COMPLAINING OF HIS MISFORTUNES

4 15/16 x 8 1/16 in.

The subject of this drawing is certainly not clear; the landlord may be describing an operation. But the simple visual evidence leaves the door open for other interpretations.

36. THE ANGEL INN AT LYMINGTON

4⅞ x 7 15/16 in.

Haniford (the name appearing in the top right corner) was the proprietor of The Angel. The name was usually spelled "Hannaford." According to local rate books the inn appears to have passed to the possession of a James Baughan in 1787.

The basic structure of the inn remains with comparatively little change.

The first draft of this drawing is on the verso of No. 38.

37. KITCHEN AT THE INN AT LYMINGTON, ON ROAD TO PILESWELL

4 15/16 x 8 in.

VERSO: *The first draft for the left portion of drawing No. 46; also a generally undecipherable inscription, "Capt Dobson [?] . . . Alum Bay . . . Cliffs fatigued ourselves . . ."*

Several inns still exist on the road along the north side of the river at Lymington on the way to Pylewell.

The drawing is reproduced in A. E. Richardson and H. Donaldson Eberlein, *The English Inn Past and Present* (London, 1925), p. 185.

38. PILESWELL, NEAR LYMINGTON IN HAMPSHIRE – THE SEAT OF ASCANIUS WILLIAM SENIOR, ESQ[RE]

4 15/16 x 15⅞ in.

VERSO LEFT-HAND SHEET: *First draft of No. 36.*

The house, now spelled "Pylewell," is on the Solent, a short distance to the north and east of Lymington. It has been considerably altered since the eighteenth century; another story has been added and the terminal pavilions removed, but the basic lines are still the same.

According to *The Victoria History of Hampshire and the Isle of Wight*, IV (London, 1911), 617, the house was purchased by Ascanius Williams, Sr., in 1781 and sold in 1787. There is, however, some evidence to indicate that the surname may have been "Senior," not "Williams." See the list of county sheriffs in William White, *History, Gazeteer and Directory of Hampshire and the Isle of Wight*, 2nd ed. (Sheffield, 1878), p. 36.

On the balloon ascent see Introduction, pp. 10-11.

39. THE OLD WHISKEY, LYMINGTON

4 15/16 x 7 15/16 in.

INSCRIBED: *"The Old Whiskey Lymington."*

VERSO: *The first draft for the left side of No. 41; inscribed "On the sea coast Pitt's Deep . . ."*

40. ROWLANDSON TALKING WITH A LADY, OUTSIDE THE "ANGEL" LYMINGTON

5 x 8 1/16 in.

41. "PITT'S DEEP," NEAR HURST CASTLE, A LITTLE ALE HOUSE FAMOUS FOR SELLING GOOD BRANDY

4⅞ x 16 in.

VERSO RIGHT-HAND SHEET: *First draft of left side of No. 32.*

The caption is inexact. Pitt's Deep is actually close to Pylewell House, to the northeast of Lymington. Hurst Castle is on the other side of the town, on the coast to the southwest. Pitt's Deep has changed extraordinarily little since Rowlandson's day. His drawing of the buildings is very accurate.

The first draft of the left side of this drawing is on the verso of No. 39.

42. SHIPPING OXEN ON BOARD THE ISLE OF WIGHT PACKET

4⅞ x 8¼ in.

This drawing is closely related to the right half of No. 44, showing the same buildings and essentially the same subject. The first draft of this drawing is on the verso of No. 44.

43. WIGSTEAD'S PARTING INTERVIEW WITH HIS LYMINGTON FRIEND

5 x 7 15/16 in.

See note to No. 34. If the identification of the friend as William Gilpin is correct, then the house would probably be Gilpin's residence, Vicar's Hill.

44. LYMINGTON QUAY, WITH THE METHOD OF SHIPPING CATTLE FOR THE ISLE OF WIGHT

4 15/16 x 16 in.

VERSO OF LEFT-HAND SHEET: *First draft of No. 42.*

45. THE PRETTY HOSTESS, AND ROWLANDSON – WITH THE EXTRAVAGANT BILL, AND WIGSTEAD

5 x 7¾ in.

46. LYMINGTON RIVER, NEAR THE QUAY – GOING ON BOARD THE VESSEL TO CARRY US TO THE ISLE OF WIGHT

4 15/16 x 15⅞ in.

INSCRIBED: *"Lymington River."*

The first draft of the left portion of this drawing is on the verso of No. 37.

47. LYMINGTON TO THE NEEDLES – ON BOARD THE PACKET

4⅞ x 8⅛ in.

The first draft of this drawing is on the verso of No. 55. See illustration facing No. 51.

48. THE QUARTER-DECK OF THE VESSEL WHICH CARRIED US TO THE NEEDLES – THE WIND BLOWING HARD

5 x 8 in.

49. SIX MILES FROM YARMOUTH – ALUM BAY

5 x 16⅛ in.

VERSO: *Coastal sketch.*

The quantity of drawings in the series devoted to the small area around the western tip of the Isle of Wight attests to Rowlandson's interest in landscape at this time and forms the climax or focus of the tour. The drawings are accurate topographically.

50. PART OF THE ROCKS IN ALUM BAY

4 13/16 x 15 15/16 in.

VERSO: *First draft, with some variations, of No. 53.*

51. THE NEEDLE ROCKS, FROM THE SEA

4 15/16 x 8 in.

VERSO: *Another view of The Needles.*

52. THE NEEDLE ROCKS

4⅞ x 16 in.

53. ST. CHRISTOPHER'S ROCK

4⅞ x 16⅛ in.

The cliff on the southern side of the western peninsula of the Isle of Wight leading to The Needles was called St. Christopher's Cliff in the eighteenth century. Richard Warner, Jr., *A Companion in a Tour round Lymington* (Southampton, [1789]), p. 137: "On passing round the Needles, a sublime scene presents itself to the eye; *St. Christopher's Cliff*, a huge chalk rock, upwards of four hundred feet in elevation, absolutely perpendicular, and excavated by the bold hand of nature into almost, a regular semicircle."

The first draft of this drawing is on the verso of No. 50.

The right-hand sheet bears a watermark very similar to that in Edward Heawood, *Watermarks* (Hilversum, Holland, 1950), No. 1849, not dated but grouped with marks of the 1760's and 1770's. Fragments of this same watermark occur on several pages. The mark "J. Whatman" that occurs on the left-hand sheet and also on several others is a countermark for the same paper.

54. [THE WESTERN END OF THE ISLE OF WIGHT FROM THE SOLENT]

4¾ x 16 in.

The caption on the mount reads "Rocks near Freshwater, in the Isle of Wight." The view, however, is not taken from Freshwater but from the vicinity of Alum Bay, showing the western end of the island, including The Needles, from the north.

55. [THE ISLE OF WIGHT AS SEEN FROM THE BLUFFS ABOVE THE NEEDLES]

4⅞ x 15⅝ in.

VERSO RIGHT-HAND SHEET: *First draft of No. 47; also an inscription over the head of the figure at the tiller, of which the only legible word is "Capt."*

The caption on the mount reads "Freshwater Bay." In fact, when Rowlandson made this drawing (which is accurate topographically), he was standing looking east on the bluffs at the western tip of the island just above The Needles. Alum Bay is in the lower left with the Solent and Hurst Castle in the left distance. St. Christopher's Rock is to the right with Scratchell's Bay below.

56. A GENERAL VIEW OF THE ISLE OF WIGHT

4 15/16 x 15⅞ in.

Probably the mouth of the Medina River at Cowes.

57. COWES HARBOUR IN THE ISLE OF WIGHT

4 15/16 x 15⅞ in.

VERSO: *Inscribed "We have now travelled . . . hundred and sixty one miles."*

A repetition of the right half of this drawing was with Frank T. Sabin in 1948. See Philip Sabin, *A Catalogue of Watercolour Drawings by Thomas Rowlandson* (an exhibition at Frank T. Sabin's galleries, London, 1948), No. 31.

58. COWES HARBOUR IN THE ISLE OF WIGHT

4 15/16 x 8 in.

59. THE BOAT WHICH WE HIRED FROM COWES TO PORTSMOUTH

4 15/16 x 7 15/16 in.

60. AT SUPPER IN PORTSMOUTH ON OUR ARRIVAL FROM COWES; ALL VERY MUCH FATIGUED

4⅞ x 7 15/16 in.

At the top, a faint pencil inscription, mostly illegible, beginning "Supper . . ."

61. GOING ON BOARD THE "HECTOR," OF 74 GUNS, LYING IN PORTSMOUTH HARBOUR

5 x 8 in.

The question of what ship it is that Rowlandson has represented is slightly complicated by the fact that there were two ships called *Hector* that figure in naval history of the early 1780's. One, a French 74, was captured at the Battle of the Saintes, April 12, 1782, but foundered off Newfoundland later that year without ever reaching England. The other *Hector* was built in 1773, served in the Channel and in the West Indies, 1777-1782, and was commissioned as a guardship at Spithead in April 1783. Thereafter she remained at various moorings in Portsmouth Harbour for several years. It appears improbable that Rowlandson would have been on board the ship before April 1783.

62. MIDDLE DECK OF THE "HECTOR," MAN-OF-WAR

4 15/16 x 16 in.

VERSO: *Landscape and seascape drawings.*

63. THE MANNER OF WORKING THE GUNS ON BOARD A SHIP IN TIME OF ACTION

5 x 8 in.

This is, of course, an imagined subject.

64. CUSTOM HOUSE CORNER, PORTSMOUTH, WITH A SMUGGLING VESSEL CUT IN TWO

4 15/16 x 15⅞ in.

INSCRIBED TO LEFT: *"Custom House Corner"; to right, "A Smuggler cutt in two this mode has been lately adopted formerly when condemned they were burnt. The present Method unfits the Vessel for future Service at the same time saving of Timber."*

VERSO: *First draft of No. 66.*

Mr. Rupert Jarvis of the Library, H. M. Customs and Excise, has suggested in a letter concerning this drawing that Rowlandson is probably referring to the statute 19 Geo. III, cap. 69 (1779). By the terms of this act officers of customs were empowered to seize and arrest any ship forfeited by the act and to secure its prosecution and condemnation. Upon legal condemnation, any such ship had hitherto been liable to be burnt or destroyed or to be used in H. M. service. Section 6 of the new act now made it lawful for the commissioners of customs "after condemnation, to direct the hull of every such ship vessel or boat to be broken up, and the materials of every such hull to be sold to the best advantage." A condemned ship was not considered "broken up" until she was at least sawn across at about amidships.

65. PORTSMOUTH POINT, WITH A DISTANT VIEW OF GOSPORT

4¾ x 16⅛ in.

WATERMARK: *J. Whatman (see note to No. 53).*

66. SPITHEAD, WITH THE EXACT SITUATION AND APPEARANCE OF THE "ROYAL GEORGE," WRECKED AUGUST 29, 1782

4 15/16 x 15⅞ in.

The *Royal George* capsized while riding at anchor at Spithead on August 29, 1782. According to Julian Slight, *A Narrative of the Loss of the Royal George*, 6th ed. (Portsea, 1843), about nine hundred people lost their lives in the disaster, many being women, children, and merchants who were visiting the vessel. The same brief account also relates (p. 29): "The masts of the Royal George remained standing out of water for several years afterwards, one of which so late as the year 1794, when it was unfortunately run down in the night by an English frigate."

The first draft of this drawing is on the verso of No. 64.

67. COTTAGES, FARNHAM, SURREY

5 x 8 in.

VERSO: *A drawing related (but not particularly closely) to right side of No. 49.*

68. AN EARTHENWARE SHOP AT FARNHAM, SURREY

4 15/16 x 7 15/16 in.

INSCRIBED AT TOP, FAINTLY, IN PENCIL: *"Farnham."*

69. ["THE TUMBLE-DOWN-DICK"]

5 x 7 15/16 in.

VERSO: *Inscribed "Mild Children Make Parents Hearts Glad M C M P H G . . ." Rowlandson then reverses the order of the initial letters to make an obscene rhyme.*

The inn sign is inscribed "Tumble Down Dick."

The caption for this drawing reads "The Post House, 'Tumble-Down-Dick,' at Alton, in Hampshire." I have not found any record of a Tumble-Down-Dick at Alton. However, according to *The Torrington Diaries* (London, 1934), I, 73, there was in 1782 an inn with this unusual name along the same road, closer to London, at Farnborough. Rowlandson may have confused the two towns. If the inn recorded in the drawing was the one at Farnborough, then this is the last drawing in the series.

APPENDIX

Transcription of "Rowlandson's Tour in a Post Chaise 1782," by J. G. [Joseph Grego],

from THE GRAPHIC SUMMER NUMBER *(1891)*

ROWLANDSON'S TOUR IN A POST CHAISE 1782

From his Studio in London to the Wreck of the "Royal George" Sunk at Spithead
(Fac-Similes of the Original Sketches, hithe[r]to unpublished)[1]

AUGUST 30, 1782, the distressing intelligence reached the Admiralty that "The Royal George," Man-of-War, the largest Ship of the royal Navy, carrying 108 guns, had, by an accident, gone down at Spithead; the Rear Admiral Kempenfelt, the Captain, (who was rescued) and Officers being on board, together with the full Crew, 370 able-bodied seamen, besides Marines & boys, and by way of visitors, over two hundred lasses, sweethearts, &c, from Portsmouth, with the wives and children of many warrant officers, & about fifty Jew-pedlars, who at the moment the totally unexpected disaster happened, were selling their wares on the middle-decks, the Sailors having just received their pay. Of the various persons on board the major part perished.

The ill-fated Man-of-War was at that time thirty years old, & had in her epoch carried with distinction the Flags of more renowned naval heroes than any Ship in the service. Admirals Lord Anson, Boscawen, Lord Rodney, and Lord Hawke, together with Rear Admiral Kempenfelt (who was writing despatches in his cabin when she sunk), had, in turn, commanded her, as the heaviest-armed and most formidable warship of the squadron. The "Royal George" unfortunately happened to be "careened" on her side, the weight of all her guns being "run" to one side, and the port-holes open, to ventilate the close quarters, when a wind struck her suddenly, and—without an instant's warning—she capsized, & immediately filled & went down, with all hands on board, settling in no great depth of water, her topmasts being visible above the waves.[2]

This deplorable disaster gave the direction to a Pic-

[1]Following is a list by number of the drawings illustrated in the article: 1, 3, 7, 8, 9, 10, 11, 12, 13, 15, 16, 20, 21, 23, 25, 26, 27 (labeled as "Barber's Shop, Alresford"), 28, 29 (labeled as "High Street, Southampton"), 30, 31, 37, 40, 41, 42, 45, 46, 49, 56, 57, 58, 61, 62, 65, 66, 68, 69. The titles Grego supplies do not differ significantly in any instance from those now on the mounts. Grego's facsimiles do not reproduce the inscriptions that occur on the drawings. One important point that is far from clear is whether all the passages Grego places in quotation marks have been transcribed from the drawings. Some of the passages are now on the drawings, but many are not (or at least are not now visible). The text of the article was not set in type but apparently was etched by hand on a series of plates. The punctuation, spelling, and syntax are very casual.

[2]There was, in fact, considerable uncertainty about the cause of the disaster. See Julian Slight, *A Narrative of the Loss of the Royal George*, 6th ed. (Portsea, 1843).

turesque Tour, undertaken by Rowlandson—(not at that time known to fame as a Caricaturist)—& Wigstead his travelling companion. These faithful comrades performed together several memorable Tours, the artist making the drawings, & Wigstead's pen furnishing the narrative, descriptions of route, & incidental details, often curious & interesting. The travelling pair planned & promptly carried out a flying visit to the wreck of the "Royal George."[3]

Rowlandson, it must be mentioned, in 1782 possessed a studio in Wardour Street, where, for five years, he had endeavoured to establish a reputation as a portrait painter, & annually exhibiting likenesses at the Royal Academy. Every stage of the present Tour was pictorially illustrated by our lively artist, who—to commence with—has represented himself in the act "of hiring the First Post Chaise." Another sketch—preliminary to their journey, depicts the pair of travellers "buying leather breeches," an indispensible item of their "fitting" equipment.

To Wigstead's share fell the post of paymaster; he is first figured busy "bargaining at a Trunkmaker's."

These preliminaries concluded we are introduced to the actual incidents of their departure. Rowlandson drew a version showing his ancient housekeeper calling him on the morning the travellers were to set off; the dame, candle in hand; is shouting to rouse the artist not yet out of bed, "Sir, Sir, Sir, its past Four o'clock." Meanwhile Wigstead has been taking an early farewell of his suburban villa,[4] and it's inmates; his horse is waiting, the owner standing by the rustic porch, assuring his sorrowing lady—"You may expect me again Sunday s'en night!" Finally the Post Chaise is pictured waiting outside Rowlandson's house in Wardour Street; Wigstead is in the act of getting in, while the artist, with his aged retainer waiting to see him off, has his foot on the doorstep, while instructing the subservient post boy as to the route.

Away, in the freshness of early morn, bowls the Post Chaise—past Piccadilly & the Parks—through Knightsbridge, & the turnpike at Kensington; splashing through the street of Brentford—notorious for its mire—& gutters monopolised by swine, thence to

> "Hounslow, whose heath sublimer terror fills,
> Shall with her gibbets lend her powder-mills"

The one lengthy street of Hounslow was, at that date, famed for bustling traffic, being accounted the first stage from London.

There were situated the great Posting Houses, when processions of Post Chaises & Coaches, & horses in end-

[3]On the probable date of the tour see Introduction, pp. 10-11.

[4]As far as is known, Wigstead was living in Gerrard Street, Soho, at the time.

less strings, were daily passing through. Rowlandson's horses were changed at the "King's Head" the Posting Inn which with "The George" divided a share of the patronage of the road. Hence sped the pilgrims; after the artist had made a sketch of the Inn Yard—which they reached at Seven O'Clock—there was no inducemen to tarry, leaving in safety the unexploded mills—(the powder had blown up with alarming effects in 1772.—Past the notorious Heath, suggestively planted out—as a timely warning to over-zealous Footpads—with gibbets, on which (festooned in chains, which clanked in the breeze) dangled the blackened remains of Knights of the Road—Highwaymen taken on the scenes of their rash exploits, or—caught elsewhere—brought back, after execution to swing, like scarecrows, on the spot they had made a terror. One Stage west of Hounslow brought the travellers through Staines, on the Salisbury highroad, over the bridge—with Runymeade meadow intervening,—to Egham on the other side of the Thames. Here Rowlandson and his friend Wigstead breakfasted in comfort, parting from the Post boy who had brought them this stage,—and who—as pictorially described by the artist—claimed their "Honours' liberal remembrances in the customary fashion before leaving.

Breakfast at Egham concluded our Travellers could not leave this rural spot without a reminiscence of "Cooper's Hill" in which is centred the local interest, full of Souvenirs of gentle Poetasters, and memories of the Denham family. Bagshot, twenty-six miles from London, with its extensive tract of heath-land, (in those times the notorious "happy hunting-ground" of Highwaymen), was the next stage from Staines.

Here our pilgrims broke their journey at "The White Hart" and—to judge from Rowlandson's Design—found the accomodation to their taste.

They were edified with the information that the place (once called Holy Hall) was formerly a residence of no less personages than the Kings of England—the royal demesne—mansion & park—being thrown open after the Civil Wars. The house was occupied by the Duke of Gloucester. Another 17 miles brought the travellers to Hook (on the Basingstoke & Odiham road), set down in their itinerary as "a village 43 miles from London"; here they "baited" at "The Spread Eagle," of which hostelery Rowlandson has left a sketch, introducing the Salisbury "stage and post." After leaving Basingstoke, an incident occurred, about seven miles therefrom at Popham Lane, "chiefly famous," says the chronicle "for the unequalled badness of the roads and the prevalence of robberies"—here, at one o'clock a delay was occasioned by a wheel getting loose, this accident happened in the hamlet or lane on the main highway where extra post boys were handy,—with assistance the wheel was finally secured, & the "Shay" covered another fourteen miles of the great western road. Stockbridge, 66 miles from London, was the next stage, the travellers traversed its one lengthy street, and cast a passing glance over "Houghton Down," where the races were then held.

In the vicinity is Danebury Hill, a spacious circular intrenchment, enclosed within high ramparts, this relic of the past, with "Woolberry"—a similar intrenchment—and "Canute's Barrow," demand a flying mention. The busy highway to the west of England is lively with traffic & Rowlandson's post boy, being of a sportive turn, enters into spirited emulation with the driver of a rival Post Chaise; the contest commences in a brisk struggle for precedence, and results in a neck & neck race over the Downs, the two "Shays" are fairly matched, the horses are urged to their utmost speed, the occupants of the respective vehicles become as excited as their postboys. Rowlandson has made a picture of the scene, besides a wonderful study of the foreshortened backs of two pairs of teams & the outriders, as viewed by the artist from the interior of his post chaise—as the carriages tear along over the Downs, swaying from side to side, risking collisions, and such trifles as the loss of a wheel or two, repeating the recent experience at Popham Lane. In this rapid fashion, without encountering total wreck, the fourteen miles intervening between Stockbridge and Salisbury are passed in a whirl, and our tearaway friends find themselves at "The White Hart"—the first Inn and chief posting-house, at Salisbury. Of the Innyard, with its turmoil of Post Chaises, Rowlandson has left a drawing. The Exeter and London Coaches started from "The White Hart"—morning, afternoon, & evening—there were arrivals & departures; there was a "Post Coach" which made the journey from Exeter to London in two days; & a "Diligence" was advertised to "carry three passengers at three-pence per mile from the "White Hart" every morning at six o'clock." There is much to be done, in the way of sightseeing, with Salisbury as headquarters. In an epitaph on Mr. Francis Hyde, a native of the place, who died Secretary to the English Embassy at Venice, the city has been—from the circumstance of its canals—favoured by a far-fetched comparison with "the Queen of the Adriatic:—

> "Born in English Venice,—thou didst die
> Dear Friend! in the Italian Salisbury."

To our Tourists, the Cathedral was the foremost attraction, and they proceeded to visit this admired edifice,—the verger conducting their inspection of its interesting features. Rowlandson produced a spirited drawing of the party assembled in the "Beauchamp Chapel" examining a noteworthy monumental effigy—a recumbent figure, clad in armour, resting on a tomb beneath a canopy. Fuller has written: "The Cathedral of Salisbury is paramount in this kind, wherein the doors and chapels equal the months, the windows the days, the pillars and pillarets of marble the hours of the year, so that all Europe affords not such an Almanack of Architecture." Our artist has left a view of the ancient "Council House and market-place," interesting from subsequent alterations. "The Market-Place"—it was written in 1780 (in view of the removal of the quaint erection figured by Rowlandson) "is very extensive and would form a beautiful square, but for the "Council-House," —which spoils the figure. This is an old Gothic wooden building; in the lower part are the Law and Crown offices & Courts; above is the Council Chamber, where the City Justices and Corporation meet." This, & "the Poultry Cross" appeared picturesque in the eyes of our friends, who subsequently adjourned to the quaint Tavern in the Market Place.

Our Travellers, being on the spot, naturally visited Salisbury Plain, and Rowlandson did not neglect the claims of Stonehenge to be represented in his Sketch Book.

Another agreeable experience led our friends to Wilton, the well-known Seat of the Earls of Pembroke, here the opportunity occurred to record the circumstance of this visit in the form of a drawing of "The Grand Room at Wilton with the traveller's lost in admiration of Vandyke's masterpiece, the gem of the famed Pembroke Collection, and one of the most note-worthy portrait-groups known to the world of art. Philip, Earl of Pembroke, rewarded Vandyke, it is related, with "five hundred Jacobuses" for this superb "Family Piece," which made the artist famous in England, and led to the patronage of Charles I & the Court. Decay, & so-called "restoration" had, at the time Rowlandson saw the picture, somewhat injured the beauty of the colouring. "In the Great Room is the celebrated Family Picture of the Pembroke's, consisting of ten whole-lengths by Vandyke; it is a perfect school of this painter. Here are two large pier-glasses, a red E[g]yptian-granite table, and one of lapis-lazuli." The room itself, "a double cube," is worthy of the treasure it contains. Having fairly seen the sights offered by Salisbury & the vicinity, our Travellers once more ordered round their Post Chaise, & paid their reckoning at the Inn,—the parting scene of the Salisbury experiences is graphically set forth by Rowlandson's hand in the drawing of their "Departure from the "White Hart," attended by the Landlord, waiters, chambermaids, Postboys, hostlers, etc. etc., who never fail attending the departure of Guests however badly they have looked after their wants during their stay." From this "note by the way" it may be fairly assumed that weighty demands were made by the Host on Wigstead's purse.

The ancient city of Southampton was full of attractions in our Travellers' eyes. It's objects of interest were approached with spirit; four drawings attest Rowlandson's industry during this part of their "Tour."

They put up at the chief Posting House "The Coach & Horses," and proceeded to "stalk the local lions"; first, as an evidence of picturesque resources, a drawing was made of "The High Street," with the moving incidents of "locomotion" on the highway, and quaint vehicles of the time, when the queerest conveyance met the view of the observer.

Thence to disport themselves amidst the fashion of the place, in company with lady friends, to the picturesque "Bar" with it's traditions of "Sir Bevis," the "patron" of Southampton. Then to sketch a view of the river, with the animated episodes of persons bathing from the boats moored on its waters. Back finally to "The Coach & Horses," where the barber attended to brush out, dress, pomatum, & powder the lengthy locks, worn in a "clubbed" *queue* at the epoch. The Post "Shay" to carry them to Lymington being in attendance meanwhile.

The Journey from Southampton to Lymington was enjoyed by our seekers for the picturesque. Warner[5] quaintly observes:—"The turnpike road which leads from Lymington to Southampton (and vice-versa) through Redbridge, is singularly beautiful. It includes about every variety of country and prospect conceivable, & extensive woods, rich savannahs, commanding eminences, and well-built villages meet the Traveller's eye in rapid succession to each other. The embattled walls of Southampton, with the distant hills of the Isle of Wight, finish the picture in a very striking manner." Lymington, favoured by its situation, it's delightful surroundings, healthy climate, and strength-giving baths,—was thus described at the time of the Tour:— "Lymington is, in a manner, insulated by the New Forest, which shuts it in on three sides; it lies in the immediate neighbourhood of the three great ports of Cowes, Southampton, & Portsmouth; yet the active spirit of its inhabitants has, by availing itself of the river,—counteracted the other apparent inconveniences of its situation,—and, without the assistance of one internal manufacturer, except salt, converted Lymington from a small & thinly inhabited place, to a populous, affluent and well-built Town. From a very early period the wines of the continent were wafted into its port, and, in succeeding ages, the small—but numerous—profits of a coasting trade have thrown into it a very considerable degree of wealth."

Our Travellers had evidently a due appreciation of

[5]Grego is referring presumably to Richard Warner, Jr. (1763-1857), an antiquarian who wrote extensively about the Lymington region. I have not located the passage cited.

the manifold attractions of Lymington, and the number of spirited drawings made by Rowlandson during their visit, attests *his* satisfaction with their quarters. The accomodation of the best hostelery (at one time kept by a widow) held out agreeable prospects, and, moreover, it was their good fortune to possess friends in the town.

First then, in order of sequence, comes a drawing of the front of "The Angel" giving on the High Street, for incident we have the artist himself, congenially engaged in chucking under the chin a pretty, buxom milkmaid, his companion & the inmates of the Inn regarding the situation with amusement. "The Kitchen of an Inn on the road to Pilewell" introduces an animated tableau, suggestive of the epoch, our Tourists figuring amongst the incidents; Wigstead is seen by the pretty barmaid, probably relating his travels of which the manuscript has yet to be discovered; a post-boy and a veteran stage-coach-driver are discussing a bowl of punch, while our limner, doubtless on simple artistic grounds, seems to be embracing an attractive handmaiden. Then there is a sketch, no less typical of the era, of the quaint old-fashioned Inn-yard of "The Angel."

On their arrival, our Sentimental pilgrims were lucky enough to meet two very charming female friends, and, in fact, the fair sex evidently enhanced the attractions of Lymington.

Wigstead had a friend there, a Clergyman, who entertained the travellers at his place, Rowlandson has made a picture of the party; and another sketch introduces the inevitable Post Chaise, with Wigstead taking leave of his host.

Our artist has left a pleasing prospect of "Mrs. Beeston's sea baths" a short distance out. Then, in the Town, we have a delightful picture, described by the artist as "A Fruit Shop," there may we view Wigstead amongst "the quality," meeting fashionable friends, & conversing with a fair personage, dressed "en Amazone." As a pendant to this version, we have Rowlandson, as the hero of a tender situation, parting from a a gentle traveller, who is seated in a chariot, stopping outside "The Angel." The rural life, and "cottages at Lymington," supplied themes for our artist, who's time seems to have been turned to great account.

An excursion was made to "Pilewell," a seat in the neighbourhood, where was viewed the very latest novelty—a balloon ascent, probably by "Vincent Lunardi," the apostle of "Aerostation"—as it was then christened.[6] The prosperity of Lymington at the date in question was, beyond its shipping trade—(of which an incident furnished Rowlandson with a couple of interesting studies) due to the circumstance that during its palmy days, the place supplied England with the useful commodity

[6]Lunardi's first ascent in England was in 1784, two years after the date suggested by Grego for the tour.

Salt. At one time forty salt-pans were at work, and £50,000 was annually paid to government, in the shape of duty, when a tax was imposed upon salt. The supply of salt from Cheshire finally extinguished this source of income. Like the majority of visitors, our friends were curious to visit the interior of a "Saltern." The process was thus explained:—the seawater is pumped into extensive reservoirs, called "salt-pans"; in these it remains, until by the effects of evaporation, the fresh particles are exhaled; the strong brine is pumped into shallow iron pans and boiled over a fierce fire until the moisture is evaporated, & salt alone remains. Rowlandson made a drawing of the interior of a "Saltern."

From Lymington our Travellers made an excursion to the famous forest; for this purpose they hired a ramshackle conveyance—a nondescript "gig," called a "*Whiskey*," "which broke down the moment Rowlandson got into it." A souvenir of the artist's visit to the New Forest survives—his drawing of "The Church, the Crown Inn, & the Duke of Gloucester's Stables at Lyndhurst."[7] The Duke, as Lord Warden of the Forest and of the Royal Manor, occupied the "King's House," where George III visited his relative on his journies between Windsor and Weymouth. In this portion of "The Tour" is set down the picture of "The Pretty Hostess"—(a youthful widow, whose personal attractions and gracious manners the artist appreciated)—"and the extravagant bill!" of which the length found not equal favour in the eyes of the alarmed Wigstead, on whom devolved the responsibility of finding the cash! After this, our friends embarked from Lymington Quay, on board a packet for the Isle of Wight. Rowlandson has left a touching picture of their experiences, crossing in a gale of wind to "The Needles."

Yarmouth afforded our artist another subject for his study. Alum Bay, six miles distant, was found no less attractive, & the effects of it's coloured sands suggested a picture. Among the rocks there, a picnic was enjoyed by the party, on the table-land, at the summit of a boulder 30 feet high, the travellers "spread their table-cloth & dined on pigeon pie, etc." Thereby refreshed, Rowlandson went to work with renewed energy, and from the extreme western point, produced a "general View of the Isle of Wight"; this excursion was fruitful in drawings; we have a panorama of "The Needles"; another version—the "Needles Rocks" from the sea; "Saint Christopher's Rock—a stupendous white cliff, said to be 500 feet perpendicular to the sea" (wrote the artist); "Freshwater Bay," & a separate study "Rocks near Freshwater." The Isle of Wight series was completed, so

[7]Grego chooses to make the visit to Lyndhurst an excursion from Lymington. In fact, however, the travelers would almost certainly pass through Lyndhurst on their way from Southampton to Lymington.

far, by the life at Cowes; we have a drawing of the Bay, and finally their departure furnished a lively picture of "Cowes Harbour, here we hired a boat to carry us to Portsmouth."

Rowlandson and Wigstead were left in the act of embarking on board the packet which was to carry them to Portsmouth. In addition to the study of "going on board," two spirited sketches were made during the passage, while the wind blew fresh "From Cowes to Portsmouth,—the boat which we hired," and a realistic picture depicting the incidents of their crossing.[8] Our friends, with additions to their party, arrived at Portsmouth, and proceeded to their hostelery to supper. Rowlandson has made a characteristic drawing of the scene, with copious consumption of punch, a custom of the time; the guests are described "as much fatigued!" The morning following all was enthusiasm and energy for sight-seeing,—there were the battle ships to be viewed, visited, and sketched. Our Artist has illustrated the incidental exertion of getting on board "The Hector," man-of-war (74 guns). Amongst the most characteristic outcomes of the experiences gained during this "Tour in search of the picturesque & the pictorial" are the more ambitious drawings executed at this stage of the journey, such as the "Middle Deck of the "*Hector*" —man-of-war, in Portsmouth Harbour." Another study was made from Gun drill, witnessed on board, "Method of working the guns on a ship in time of action; the artist supplying the tragic details from what was described by the gunners.

Equally in Rowlandson's best vein is the lively drawing of "Portsmouth Point, with a distant view of Gosport"; a companion version represents "Custom House Corner," with, as local incidents, on the one side, sailors and Portsmouth lasses romping, dancing, & revelling, after the traditions of their Kind; on the other side is a smuggler cutter in two, having been captured and condemned by the officers of the customs, smuggling being a popular trade, but liable to reverses, even in those free-and-easy days.

Spithead, the aim & ultimate object of their travels, is at last reached, and to the series of drawings which form the animated record of the "Tour to the Wreck of 'The Royal George,'" Rowlandson was enabled to add a veracious drawing of what was at that time visible of the unfortunate ship, once the pride of the British Navy. The huge man-of-war had righted herself in sinking, and, in settling down in her final resting-place, remained as if in dock; the masts & upper gear being alone above the shallow waters in which so many unfortunates had perished, when the ship foundered with all hands.

[8]Grego evidently places drawing No. 48 between Cowes and Portsmouth rather than Lymington and The Needles.

Experiments were shortly made with the diving-bell, several of her guns were got out, and brought to shore, but, owing to her enormous weight, it was impossible to raise the ship; moreover, it was stated by one of her carpenters (who had escaped from the catastrophy) that her timbers were perishing from rot, & would afford no purchase. With a farewell glance at the erst victorious and formidable leviathan, our Tourists resumed their route, travelling townwards. Alresford presented picturesque materials for a study on the homeward journey.[9] At "Alton post-house," the sign-board "Tumble-down Dick" (originally set up to ridicule the rapid fall of Richard Cromwell), was pictorially noted-down. "An Earthenware Shop, at Farnham, with a village on the road, furnished versions of the quaint old-world buildings, which were common at that date. Rowlandson, to conclude his series of drawings, produced an appropriate Tailpiece from nature, (literally the tails of their post-horses) and thus finished off the lately-discovered, "long-lost" "Picturesque Tour in a Post Chaise."

J. G.

[9] See note to No. 27.